C-213

CAREER EXAMINATION SERIES

THIS IS YOUR **PASSBOOK**® FOR ...

DISPATCHER

NLC®

NATIONAL LEARNING CORPORATION®
passbooks.com

PASSBOOK® SERIES

THE *PASSBOOK® SERIES* has been created to prepare applicants and candidates for the ultimate academic battlefield – the examination room.

At some time in our lives, each and every one of us may be required to take an examination – for validation, matriculation, admission, qualification, registration, certification, or licensure.

Based on the assumption that every applicant or candidate has met the basic formal educational standards, has taken the required number of courses, and read the necessary texts, the *PASSBOOK® SERIES* furnishes the one special preparation which may assure passing with confidence, instead of failing with insecurity. Examination questions – together with answers – are furnished as the basic vehicle for study so that the mysteries of the examination and its compounding difficulties may be eliminated or diminished by a sure method.

This book is meant to help you pass your examination provided that you qualify and are serious in your objective.

The entire field is reviewed through the huge store of content information which is succinctly presented through a provocative and challenging approach – the question-and-answer method.

A climate of success is established by furnishing the correct answers at the end of each test.

You soon learn to recognize types of questions, forms of questions, and patterns of questioning. You may even begin to anticipate expected outcomes.

You perceive that many questions are repeated or adapted so that you can gain acute insights, which may enable you to score many sure points.

You learn how to confront new questions, or types of questions, and to attack them confidently and work out the correct answers.

You note objectives and emphases, and recognize pitfalls and dangers, so that you may make positive educational adjustments.

Moreover, you are kept fully informed in relation to new concepts, methods, practices, and directions in the field.

You discover that you arre actually taking the examination all the time: you are preparing for the examination by "taking" an examination, not by reading extraneous and/or supererogatory textbooks.

In short, this PASSBOOK®, used directedly, should be an important factor in helping you to pass your test.

DISPATCHER

DUTIES

Operates radio equipment to dispatch police officers, fire personnel, EMS personnel, animal control officers and other emergency vehicles to scenes of crimes, accidents, fires or other emergencies; answers incoming telephone calls and provides information or receives complaints from the public; maintains continuous status and location records of police, fire and emergency vehicles; maintains security and order of the control area; keeps listings of telephone numbers and other necessary information up to date; may operate teletype machine and computer-aided equipment to secure and transmit information; may monitor police, fire and citizen band frequencies; records and files complaints and accident reports and additional routine clerical duties; periodically checks correct operation of radio and telephone equipment to insure continuity of service; maintains a daily log of calls received and transmitted; may type a variety of routine correspondence and reports.

SCOPE OF THE EXAMINATION

The written test will cover knowledge, skills and/or abilities in such areas as:

1. Coding/decoding information;
2. Following directions (maps);
3. Retaining and comprehending spoken information from calls for emergency services;
4. Name and number checking; and
5. Understanding and interpreting written material.

HOW TO TAKE A TEST

I. YOU MUST PASS AN EXAMINATION

A. *WHAT EVERY CANDIDATE SHOULD KNOW*

Examination applicants often ask us for help in preparing for the written test. What can I study in advance? What kinds of questions will be asked? How will the test be given? How will the papers be graded?

As an applicant for a civil service examination, you may be wondering about some of these things. Our purpose here is to suggest effective methods of advance study and to describe civil service examinations.

Your chances for success on this examination can be increased if you know how to prepare. Those "pre-examination jitters" can be reduced if you know what to expect. You can even experience an adventure in good citizenship if you know why civil service exams are given.

B. *WHY ARE CIVIL SERVICE EXAMINATIONS GIVEN?*

Civil service examinations are important to you in two ways. As a citizen, you want public jobs filled by employees who know how to do their work. As a job seeker, you want a fair chance to compete for that job on an equal footing with other candidates. The best-known means of accomplishing this two-fold goal is the competitive examination.

Exams are widely publicized throughout the nation. They may be administered for jobs in federal, state, city, municipal, town or village governments or agencies.

Any citizen may apply, with some limitations, such as the age or residence of applicants. Your experience and education may be reviewed to see whether you meet the requirements for the particular examination. When these requirements exist, they are reasonable and applied consistently to all applicants. Thus, a competitive examination may cause you some uneasiness now, but it is your privilege and safeguard.

C. *HOW ARE CIVIL SERVICE EXAMS DEVELOPED?*

Examinations are carefully written by trained technicians who are specialists in the field known as "psychological measurement," in consultation with recognized authorities in the field of work that the test will cover. These experts recommend the subject matter areas or skills to be tested; only those knowledges or skills important to your success on the job are included. The most reliable books and source materials available are used as references. Together, the experts and technicians judge the difficulty level of the questions.

Test technicians know how to phrase questions so that the problem is clearly stated. Their ethics do not permit "trick" or "catch" questions. Questions may have been tried out on sample groups, or subjected to statistical analysis, to determine their usefulness.

Written tests are often used in combination with performance tests, ratings of training and experience, and oral interviews. All of these measures combine to form the best-known means of finding the right person for the right job.

II. HOW TO PASS THE WRITTEN TEST

A. NATURE OF THE EXAMINATION

To prepare intelligently for civil service examinations, you should know how they differ from school examinations you have taken. In school you were assigned certain definite pages to read or subjects to cover. The examination questions were quite detailed and usually emphasized memory. Civil service exams, on the other hand, try to discover your present ability to perform the duties of a position, plus your potentiality to learn these duties. In other words, a civil service exam attempts to predict how successful you will be. Questions cover such a broad area that they cannot be as minute and detailed as school exam questions.

In the public service similar kinds of work, or positions, are grouped together in one "class." This process is known as *position-classification*. All the positions in a class are paid according to the salary range for that class. One class title covers all of these positions, and they are all tested by the same examination.

B. FOUR BASIC STEPS

1) Study the announcement

How, then, can you know what subjects to study? Our best answer is: "Learn as much as possible about the class of positions for which you've applied." The exam will test the knowledge, skills and abilities needed to do the work.

Your most valuable source of information about the position you want is the official exam announcement. This announcement lists the training and experience qualifications. Check these standards and apply only if you come reasonably close to meeting them.

The brief description of the position in the examination announcement offers some clues to the subjects which will be tested. Think about the job itself. Review the duties in your mind. Can you perform them, or are there some in which you are rusty? Fill in the blank spots in your preparation.

Many jurisdictions preview the written test in the exam announcement by including a section called "Knowledge and Abilities Required," "Scope of the Examination," or some similar heading. Here you will find out specifically what fields will be tested.

2) Review your own background

Once you learn in general what the position is all about, and what you need to know to do the work, ask yourself which subjects you already know fairly well and which need improvement. You may wonder whether to concentrate on improving your strong areas or on building some background in your fields of weakness. When the announcement has specified "some knowledge" or "considerable knowledge," or has used adjectives like "beginning principles of…" or "advanced … methods," you can get a clue as to the number and difficulty of questions to be asked in any given field. More questions, and hence broader coverage, would be included for those subjects which are more important in the work. Now weigh your strengths and weaknesses against the job requirements and prepare accordingly.

3) Determine the level of the position

Another way to tell how intensively you should prepare is to understand the level of the job for which you are applying. Is it the entering level? In other words, is this the position in which beginners in a field of work are hired? Or is it an intermediate or advanced level? Sometimes this is indicated by such words as "Junior" or "Senior" in the class title. Other jurisdictions use Roman numerals to designate the level – Clerk I, Clerk II, for example. The word "Supervisor" sometimes appears in the title. If the level is not indicated by the title, check the description of duties. Will you be working under very close supervision, or will you have responsibility for independent decisions in this work?

4) Choose appropriate study materials

Now that you know the subjects to be examined and the relative amount of each subject to be covered, you can choose suitable study materials. For beginning level jobs, or even advanced ones, if you have a pronounced weakness in some aspect of your training, read a modern, standard textbook in that field. Be sure it is up to date and has general coverage. Such books are normally available at your library, and the librarian will be glad to help you locate one. For entry-level positions, questions of appropriate difficulty are chosen – neither highly advanced questions, nor those too simple. Such questions require careful thought but not advanced training.

If the position for which you are applying is technical or advanced, you will read more advanced, specialized material. If you are already familiar with the basic principles of your field, elementary textbooks would waste your time. Concentrate on advanced textbooks and technical periodicals. Think through the concepts and review difficult problems in your field.

These are all general sources. You can get more ideas on your own initiative, following these leads. For example, training manuals and publications of the government agency which employs workers in your field can be useful, particularly for technical and professional positions. A letter or visit to the government department involved may result in more specific study suggestions, and certainly will provide you with a more definite idea of the exact nature of the position you are seeking.

III. KINDS OF TESTS

Tests are used for purposes other than measuring knowledge and ability to perform specified duties. For some positions, it is equally important to test ability to make adjustments to new situations or to profit from training. In others, basic mental abilities not dependent on information are essential. Questions which test these things may not appear as pertinent to the duties of the position as those which test for knowledge and information. Yet they are often highly important parts of a fair examination. For very general questions, it is almost impossible to help you direct your study efforts. What we can do is to point out some of the more common of these general abilities needed in public service positions and describe some typical questions.

1) General information

Broad, general information has been found useful for predicting job success in some kinds of work. This is tested in a variety of ways, from vocabulary lists to questions about current events. Basic background in some field of work, such as sociology or economics, may be sampled in a group of questions. Often these are principles which have become familiar to most persons through exposure rather than through formal training. It is difficult to advise you how to study for these questions; being alert to the world around you is our best suggestion.

2) Verbal ability

An example of an ability needed in many positions is verbal or language ability. Verbal ability is, in brief, the ability to use and understand words. Vocabulary and grammar tests are typical measures of this ability. Reading comprehension or paragraph interpretation questions are common in many kinds of civil service tests. You are given a paragraph of written material and asked to find its central meaning.

3) Numerical ability

Number skills can be tested by the familiar arithmetic problem, by checking paired lists of numbers to see which are alike and which are different, or by interpreting charts and graphs. In the latter test, a graph may be printed in the test booklet which you are asked to use as the basis for answering questions.

4) Observation

A popular test for law-enforcement positions is the observation test. A picture is shown to you for several minutes, then taken away. Questions about the picture test your ability to observe both details and larger elements.

5) Following directions

In many positions in the public service, the employee must be able to carry out written instructions dependably and accurately. You may be given a chart with several columns, each column listing a variety of information. The questions require you to carry out directions involving the information given in the chart.

6) Skills and aptitudes

Performance tests effectively measure some manual skills and aptitudes. When the skill is one in which you are trained, such as typing or shorthand, you can practice. These tests are often very much like those given in business school or high school courses. For many of the other skills and aptitudes, however, no short-time preparation can be made. Skills and abilities natural to you or that you have developed throughout your lifetime are being tested.

Many of the general questions just described provide all the data needed to answer the questions and ask you to use your reasoning ability to find the answers. Your best preparation for these tests, as well as for tests of facts and ideas, is to be at your physical and mental best. You, no doubt, have your own methods of getting into an exam-taking mood and keeping "in shape." The next section lists some ideas on this subject.

IV. KINDS OF QUESTIONS

Only rarely is the "essay" question, which you answer in narrative form, used in civil service tests. Civil service tests are usually of the short-answer type. Full instructions for answering these questions will be given to you at the examination. But in case this is your first experience with short-answer questions and separate answer sheets, here is what you need to know:

1) Multiple-choice Questions

Most popular of the short-answer questions is the "multiple choice" or "best answer" question. It can be used, for example, to test for factual knowledge, ability to solve problems or judgment in meeting situations found at work.

A multiple-choice question is normally one of three types—

- It can begin with an incomplete statement followed by several possible endings. You are to find the one ending which *best* completes the statement, although some of the others may not be entirely wrong.
- It can also be a complete statement in the form of a question which is answered by choosing one of the statements listed.
- It can be in the form of a problem – again you select the best answer.

Here is an example of a multiple-choice question with a discussion which should give you some clues as to the method for choosing the right answer:

When an employee has a complaint about his assignment, the action which will *best* help him overcome his difficulty is to
   A. discuss his difficulty with his coworkers
   B. take the problem to the head of the organization
   C. take the problem to the person who gave him the assignment
   D. say nothing to anyone about his complaint

In answering this question, you should study each of the choices to find which is best. Consider choice "A" – Certainly an employee may discuss his complaint with fellow employees, but no change or improvement can result, and the complaint remains unresolved. Choice "B" is a poor choice since the head of the organization probably does not know what assignment you have been given, and taking your problem to him is known as "going over the head" of the supervisor. The supervisor, or person who made the assignment, is the person who can clarify it or correct any injustice. Choice "C" is, therefore, correct. To say nothing, as in choice "D," is unwise. Supervisors have and interest in knowing the problems employees are facing, and the employee is seeking a solution to his problem.

2) True/False Questions

The "true/false" or "right/wrong" form of question is sometimes used. Here a complete statement is given. Your job is to decide whether the statement is right or wrong.

SAMPLE: A roaming cell-phone call to a nearby city costs less than a non-roaming call to a distant city.

This statement is wrong, or false, since roaming calls are more expensive.
This is not a complete list of all possible question forms, although most of the others are variations of these common types. You will always get complete directions for

answering questions. Be sure you understand *how* to mark your answers – ask questions until you do.

V. RECORDING YOUR ANSWERS

Computer terminals are used more and more today for many different kinds of exams.

For an examination with very few applicants, you may be told to record your answers in the test booklet itself. Separate answer sheets are much more common. If this separate answer sheet is to be scored by machine – and this is often the case – it is highly important that you mark your answers correctly in order to get credit.

An electronic scoring machine is often used in civil service offices because of the speed with which papers can be scored. Machine-scored answer sheets must be marked with a pencil, which will be given to you. This pencil has a high graphite content which responds to the electronic scoring machine. As a matter of fact, stray dots may register as answers, so do not let your pencil rest on the answer sheet while you are pondering the correct answer. Also, if your pencil lead breaks or is otherwise defective, ask for another.

Since the answer sheet will be dropped in a slot in the scoring machine, be careful not to bend the corners or get the paper crumpled.

The answer sheet normally has five vertical columns of numbers, with 30 numbers to a column. These numbers correspond to the question numbers in your test booklet. After each number, going across the page are four or five pairs of dotted lines. These short dotted lines have small letters or numbers above them. The first two pairs may also have a "T" or "F" above the letters. This indicates that the first two pairs only are to be used if the questions are of the true-false type. If the questions are multiple choice, disregard the "T" and "F" and pay attention only to the small letters or numbers.

Answer your questions in the manner of the sample that follows:

> 32. The largest city in the United States is
>   A. Washington, D.C.
>   B. New York City
>   C. Chicago
>   D. Detroit
>   E. San Francisco

> 1) Choose the answer you think is best. (New York City is the largest, so "B" is correct.)
> 2) Find the row of dotted lines numbered the same as the question you are answering. (Find row number 32)
> 3) Find the pair of dotted lines corresponding to the answer. (Find the pair of lines under the mark "B.")
> 4) Make a solid black mark between the dotted lines.

VI. BEFORE THE TEST

Common sense will help you find procedures to follow to get ready for an examination. Too many of us, however, overlook these sensible measures. Indeed, nervousness and fatigue have been found to be the most serious reasons why applicants fail to do their best on civil service tests. Here is a list of reminders:

- Begin your preparation early – Don't wait until the last minute to go scurrying around for books and materials or to find out what the position is all about.
- Prepare continuously – An hour a night for a week is better than an all-night cram session. This has been definitely established. What is more, a night a week for a month will return better dividends than crowding your study into a shorter period of time.
- Locate the place of the exam – You have been sent a notice telling you when and where to report for the examination. If the location is in a different town or otherwise unfamiliar to you, it would be well to inquire the best route and learn something about the building.
- Relax the night before the test – Allow your mind to rest. Do not study at all that night. Plan some mild recreation or diversion; then go to bed early and get a good night's sleep.
- Get up early enough to make a leisurely trip to the place for the test – This way unforeseen events, traffic snarls, unfamiliar buildings, etc. will not upset you.
- Dress comfortably – A written test is not a fashion show. You will be known by number and not by name, so wear something comfortable.
- Leave excess paraphernalia at home – Shopping bags and odd bundles will get in your way. You need bring only the items mentioned in the official notice you received; usually everything you need is provided. Do not bring reference books to the exam. They will only confuse those last minutes and be taken away from you when in the test room.
- Arrive somewhat ahead of time – If because of transportation schedules you must get there very early, bring a newspaper or magazine to take your mind off yourself while waiting.
- Locate the examination room – When you have found the proper room, you will be directed to the seat or part of the room where you will sit. Sometimes you are given a sheet of instructions to read while you are waiting. Do not fill out any forms until you are told to do so; just read them and be prepared.
- Relax and prepare to listen to the instructions
- If you have any physical problem that may keep you from doing your best, be sure to tell the test administrator. If you are sick or in poor health, you really cannot do your best on the exam. You can come back and take the test some other time.

VII. AT THE TEST

The day of the test is here and you have the test booklet in your hand. The temptation to get going is very strong. Caution! There is more to success than knowing the right answers. You must know how to identify your papers and understand variations in the type of short-answer question used in this particular examination. Follow these suggestions for maximum results from your efforts:

1) Cooperate with the monitor

The test administrator has a duty to create a situation in which you can be as much at ease as possible. He will give instructions, tell you when to begin, check to see that you are marking your answer sheet correctly, and so on. He is not there to guard you, although he will see that your competitors do not take unfair advantage. He wants to help you do your best.

2) Listen to all instructions

Don't jump the gun! Wait until you understand all directions. In most civil service tests you get more time than you need to answer the questions. So don't be in a hurry. Read each word of instructions until you clearly understand the meaning. Study the examples, listen to all announcements and follow directions. Ask questions if you do not understand what to do.

3) Identify your papers

Civil service exams are usually identified by number only. You will be assigned a number; you must not put your name on your test papers. Be sure to copy your number correctly. Since more than one exam may be given, copy your exact examination title.

4) Plan your time

Unless you are told that a test is a "speed" or "rate of work" test, speed itself is usually not important. Time enough to answer all the questions will be provided, but this does not mean that you have all day. An overall time limit has been set. Divide the total time (in minutes) by the number of questions to determine the approximate time you have for each question.

5) Do not linger over difficult questions

If you come across a difficult question, mark it with a paper clip (useful to have along) and come back to it when you have been through the booklet. One caution if you do this – be sure to skip a number on your answer sheet as well. Check often to be sure that you have not lost your place and that you are marking in the row numbered the same as the question you are answering.

6) Read the questions

Be sure you know what the question asks! Many capable people are unsuccessful because they failed to *read* the questions correctly.

7) Answer all questions

Unless you have been instructed that a penalty will be deducted for incorrect answers, it is better to guess than to omit a question.

8) Speed tests

It is often better NOT to guess on speed tests. It has been found that on timed tests people are tempted to spend the last few seconds before time is called in marking answers at random – without even reading them – in the hope of picking up a few extra points. To discourage this practice, the instructions may warn you that your score will be "corrected" for guessing. That is, a penalty will be applied. The incorrect answers will be deducted from the correct ones, or some other penalty formula will be used.

9) Review your answers

If you finish before time is called, go back to the questions you guessed or omitted to give them further thought. Review other answers if you have time.

10) Return your test materials

If you are ready to leave before others have finished or time is called, take ALL your materials to the monitor and leave quietly. Never take any test material with you. The monitor can discover whose papers are not complete, and taking a test booklet may be grounds for disqualification.

VIII. EXAMINATION TECHNIQUES

1) Read the general instructions carefully. These are usually printed on the first page of the exam booklet. As a rule, these instructions refer to the timing of the examination; the fact that you should not start work until the signal and must stop work at a signal, etc. If there are any *special* instructions, such as a choice of questions to be answered, make sure that you note this instruction carefully.

2) When you are ready to start work on the examination, that is as soon as the signal has been given, read the instructions to each question booklet, underline any key words or phrases, such as *least, best, outline, describe* and the like. In this way you will tend to answer as requested rather than discover on reviewing your paper that you *listed without describing*, that you selected the *worst* choice rather than the *best* choice, etc.

3) If the examination is of the objective or multiple-choice type – that is, each question will also give a series of possible answers: A, B, C or D, and you are called upon to select the best answer and write the letter next to that answer on your answer paper – it is advisable to start answering each question in turn. There may be anywhere from 50 to 100 such questions in the three or four hours allotted and you can see how much time would be taken if you read through all the questions before beginning to answer any. Furthermore, if you come across a question or group of questions which you know would be difficult to answer, it would undoubtedly affect your handling of all the other questions.

4) If the examination is of the essay type and contains but a few questions, it is a moot point as to whether you should read all the questions before starting to answer any one. Of course, if you are given a choice – say five out of seven and the like – then it is essential to read all the questions so you can eliminate the two that are most difficult. If, however, you are asked to answer all the questions, there may be danger in trying to answer the easiest one first because you may find that you will spend too much time on it. The best technique is to answer the first question, then proceed to the second, etc.

5) Time your answers. Before the exam begins, write down the time it started, then add the time allowed for the examination and write down the time it must be completed, then divide the time available somewhat as follows:

- If 3-1/2 hours are allowed, that would be 210 minutes. If you have 80 objective-type questions, that would be an average of 2-1/2 minutes per question. Allow yourself no more than 2 minutes per question, or a total of 160 minutes, which will permit about 50 minutes to review.
- If for the time allotment of 210 minutes there are 7 essay questions to answer, that would average about 30 minutes a question. Give yourself only 25 minutes per question so that you have about 35 minutes to review.

6) The most important instruction is to *read each question* and make sure you know what is wanted. The second most important instruction is to *time yourself properly* so that you answer every question. The third most important instruction is to *answer every question*. Guess if you have to but include something for each question. Remember that you will receive no credit for a blank and will probably receive some credit if you write something in answer to an essay question. If you guess a letter – say "B" for a multiple-choice question – you may have guessed right. If you leave a blank as an answer to a multiple-choice question, the examiners may respect your feelings but it will not add a point to your score. Some exams may penalize you for wrong answers, so in such cases *only*, you may not want to guess unless you have some basis for your answer.

7) Suggestions
   a. Objective-type questions
      1. Examine the question booklet for proper sequence of pages and questions
      2. Read all instructions carefully
      3. Skip any question which seems too difficult; return to it after all other questions have been answered
      4. Apportion your time properly; do not spend too much time on any single question or group of questions
      5. Note and underline key words – *all, most, fewest, least, best, worst, same, opposite,* etc.
      6. Pay particular attention to negatives
      7. Note unusual option, e.g., unduly long, short, complex, different or similar in content to the body of the question
      8. Observe the use of "hedging" words – *probably, may, most likely,* etc.
      9. Make sure that your answer is put next to the same number as the question
      10. Do not second-guess unless you have good reason to believe the second answer is definitely more correct
      11. Cross out original answer if you decide another answer is more accurate; do not erase until you are ready to hand your paper in
      12. Answer all questions; guess unless instructed otherwise
      13. Leave time for review

   b. Essay questions
      1. Read each question carefully
      2. Determine exactly what is wanted. Underline key words or phrases.
      3. Decide on outline or paragraph answer

4. Include many different points and elements unless asked to develop any one or two points or elements
5. Show impartiality by giving pros and cons unless directed to select one side only
6. Make and write down any assumptions you find necessary to answer the questions
7. Watch your English, grammar, punctuation and choice of words
8. Time your answers; don't crowd material

8) Answering the essay question

Most essay questions can be answered by framing the specific response around several key words or ideas. Here are a few such key words or ideas:

M's: manpower, materials, methods, money, management
P's: purpose, program, policy, plan, procedure, practice, problems, pitfalls, personnel, public relations

  a. Six basic steps in handling problems:
   1. Preliminary plan and background development
   2. Collect information, data and facts
   3. Analyze and interpret information, data and facts
   4. Analyze and develop solutions as well as make recommendations
   5. Prepare report and sell recommendations
   6. Install recommendations and follow up effectiveness

  b. Pitfalls to avoid
   1. *Taking things for granted* – A statement of the situation does not necessarily imply that each of the elements is necessarily true; for example, a complaint may be invalid and biased so that all that can be taken for granted is that a complaint has been registered
   2. *Considering only one side of a situation* – Wherever possible, indicate several alternatives and then point out the reasons you selected the best one
   3. *Failing to indicate follow up* – Whenever your answer indicates action on your part, make certain that you will take proper follow-up action to see how successful your recommendations, procedures or actions turn out to be
   4. *Taking too long in answering any single question* – Remember to time your answers properly

IX. AFTER THE TEST

Scoring procedures differ in detail among civil service jurisdictions although the general principles are the same. Whether the papers are hand-scored or graded by machine we have described, they are nearly always graded by number. That is, the person who marks the paper knows only the number – never the name – of the applicant. Not until all the papers have been graded will they be matched with names. If other tests, such as training and experience or oral interview ratings have been given, scores will be combined. Different parts of the examination usually have different weights. For example, the written test might count 60 percent of the final grade, and a rating of training and experience 40 percent. In many jurisdictions, veterans will have a certain number of points added to their grades.

After the final grade has been determined, the names are placed in grade order and an eligible list is established. There are various methods for resolving ties between those who get the same final grade – probably the most common is to place first the name of the person whose application was received first. Job offers are made from the eligible list in the order the names appear on it. You will be notified of your grade and your rank as soon as all these computations have been made. This will be done as rapidly as possible.

People who are found to meet the requirements in the announcement are called "eligibles." Their names are put on a list of eligible candidates. An eligible's chances of getting a job depend on how high he stands on this list and how fast agencies are filling jobs from the list.

When a job is to be filled from a list of eligibles, the agency asks for the names of people on the list of eligibles for that job. When the civil service commission receives this request, it sends to the agency the names of the three people highest on this list. Or, if the job to be filled has specialized requirements, the office sends the agency the names of the top three persons who meet these requirements from the general list.

The appointing officer makes a choice from among the three people whose names were sent to him. If the selected person accepts the appointment, the names of the others are put back on the list to be considered for future openings.

That is the rule in hiring from all kinds of eligible lists, whether they are for typist, carpenter, chemist, or something else. For every vacancy, the appointing officer has his choice of any one of the top three eligibles on the list. This explains why the person whose name is on top of the list sometimes does not get an appointment when some of the persons lower on the list do. If the appointing officer chooses the second or third eligible, the No. 1 eligible does not get a job at once, but stays on the list until he is appointed or the list is terminated.

X. HOW TO PASS THE INTERVIEW TEST

The examination for which you applied requires an oral interview test. You have already taken the written test and you are now being called for the interview test – the final part of the formal examination.

You may think that it is not possible to prepare for an interview test and that there are no procedures to follow during an interview. Our purpose is to point out some things you can do in advance that will help you and some good rules to follow and pitfalls to avoid while you are being interviewed.

What is an interview supposed to test?

The written examination is designed to test the technical knowledge and competence of the candidate; the oral is designed to evaluate intangible qualities, not readily measured otherwise, and to establish a list showing the relative fitness of each candidate – as measured against his competitors – for the position sought. Scoring is not on the basis of "right" and "wrong," but on a sliding scale of values ranging from "not passable" to "outstanding." As a matter of fact, it is possible to achieve a relatively low score without a single "incorrect" answer because of evident weakness in the qualities being measured.

Occasionally, an examination may consist entirely of an oral test – either an individual or a group oral. In such cases, information is sought concerning the technical knowledges and abilities of the candidate, since there has been no written examination for this purpose. More commonly, however, an oral test is used to supplement a written examination.

Who conducts interviews?

The composition of oral boards varies among different jurisdictions. In nearly all, a representative of the personnel department serves as chairman. One of the members of the board may be a representative of the department in which the candidate would work. In some cases, "outside experts" are used, and, frequently, a businessman or some other representative of the general public is asked to serve. Labor and management or other special groups may be represented. The aim is to secure the services of experts in the appropriate field.

However the board is composed, it is a good idea (and not at all improper or unethical) to ascertain in advance of the interview who the members are and what groups they represent. When you are introduced to them, you will have some idea of their backgrounds and interests, and at least you will not stutter and stammer over their names.

What should be done before the interview?

While knowledge about the board members is useful and takes some of the surprise element out of the interview, there is other preparation which is more substantive. It *is* possible to prepare for an oral interview – in several ways:

1) Keep a copy of your application and review it carefully before the interview

This may be the only document before the oral board, and the starting point of the interview. Know what education and experience you have listed there, and the sequence and dates of all of it. Sometimes the board will ask you to review the highlights of your experience for them; you should not have to hem and haw doing it.

2) Study the class specification and the examination announcement

Usually, the oral board has one or both of these to guide them. The qualities, characteristics or knowledges required by the position sought are stated in these documents. They offer valuable clues as to the nature of the oral interview. For example, if the job involves supervisory responsibilities, the announcement will usually indicate that knowledge of modern supervisory methods and the qualifications of the candidate as a supervisor will be tested. If so, you can expect such questions, frequently in the form of a hypothetical situation which you are expected to solve. NEVER go into an oral without knowledge of the duties and responsibilities of the job you seek.

3) Think through each qualification required

Try to visualize the kind of questions you would ask if you were a board member. How well could you answer them? Try especially to appraise your own knowledge and background in each area, *measured against the job sought*, and identify any areas in which you are weak. Be critical and realistic – do not flatter yourself.

4) Do some general reading in areas in which you feel you may be weak

For example, if the job involves supervision and your past experience has NOT, some general reading in supervisory methods and practices, particularly in the field of human relations, might be useful. Do NOT study agency procedures or detailed manuals. The oral board will be testing your understanding and capacity, not your memory.

5) Get a good night's sleep and watch your general health and mental attitude

You will want a clear head at the interview. Take care of a cold or any other minor ailment, and of course, no hangovers.

What should be done on the day of the interview?

Now comes the day of the interview itself. Give yourself plenty of time to get there. Plan to arrive somewhat ahead of the scheduled time, particularly if your appointment is in the fore part of the day. If a previous candidate fails to appear, the board might be ready for you a bit early. By early afternoon an oral board is almost invariably behind schedule if there are many candidates, and you may have to wait. Take along a book or magazine to read, or your application to review, but leave any extraneous material in the waiting room when you go in for your interview. In any event, relax and compose yourself.

The matter of dress is important. The board is forming impressions about you – from your experience, your manners, your attitude, and your appearance. Give your personal appearance careful attention. Dress your best, but not your flashiest. Choose conservative, appropriate clothing, and be sure it is immaculate. This is a business interview, and your appearance should indicate that you regard it as such. Besides, being well groomed and properly dressed will help boost your confidence.

Sooner or later, someone will call your name and escort you into the interview room. *This is it.* From here on you are on your own. It is too late for any more preparation. But remember, you asked for this opportunity to prove your fitness, and you are here because your request was granted.

What happens when you go in?

The usual sequence of events will be as follows: The clerk (who is often the board stenographer) will introduce you to the chairman of the oral board, who will introduce you to the other members of the board. Acknowledge the introductions before you sit down. Do not be surprised if you find a microphone facing you or a stenotypist sitting by. Oral interviews are usually recorded in the event of an appeal or other review.

Usually the chairman of the board will open the interview by reviewing the highlights of your education and work experience from your application – primarily for the benefit of the other members of the board, as well as to get the material into the record. Do not interrupt or comment unless there is an error or significant misinterpretation; if that is the case, do not hesitate. But do not quibble about insignificant matters. Also, he will usually ask you some question about your education, experience or your present job – partly to get you to start talking and to establish the interviewing "rapport." He may start the actual questioning, or turn it over to one of the other members. Frequently, each member undertakes the questioning on a particular area, one in which he is perhaps most competent, so you can expect each member to participate in the examination. Because time is limited, you may also expect some rather abrupt switches in the direction the questioning takes, so do not be upset by it. Normally, a board member will not pursue a single line of questioning unless he discovers a particular strength or weakness.

After each member has participated, the chairman will usually ask whether any member has any further questions, then will ask you if you have anything you wish to add. Unless you are expecting this question, it may floor you. Worse, it may start you off on an extended, extemporaneous speech. The board is not usually seeking more information. The question is principally to offer you a last opportunity to present further qualifications or to indicate that you have nothing to add. So, if you feel that a significant qualification or characteristic has been overlooked, it is proper to point it out in a sentence or so. Do not compliment the board on the thoroughness of their examination – they have been sketchy, and you know it. If you wish, merely say, "No thank you, I have nothing further to add." This is a point where you can "talk yourself out" of a good impression or fail to present an important bit of information. Remember, *you close the interview yourself.*

The chairman will then say, "That is all, Mr. _____, thank you." Do not be startled; the interview is over, and quicker than you think. Thank him, gather your belongings and take your leave. Save your sigh of relief for the other side of the door.

How to put your best foot forward

Throughout this entire process, you may feel that the board individually and collectively is trying to pierce your defenses, seek out your hidden weaknesses and embarrass and confuse you. Actually, this is not true. They are obliged to make an appraisal of your qualifications for the job you are seeking, and they want to see you in your best light. Remember, they must interview all candidates and a non-cooperative candidate may become a failure in spite of their best efforts to bring out his qualifications. Here are 15 suggestions that will help you:

1) Be natural – Keep your attitude confident, not cocky

If you are not confident that you can do the job, do not expect the board to be. Do not apologize for your weaknesses, try to bring out your strong points. The board is interested in a positive, not negative, presentation. Cockiness will antagonize any board member and make him wonder if you are covering up a weakness by a false show of strength.

2) Get comfortable, but don't lounge or sprawl

Sit erectly but not stiffly. A careless posture may lead the board to conclude that you are careless in other things, or at least that you are not impressed by the importance of the occasion. Either conclusion is natural, even if incorrect. Do not fuss with your clothing, a pencil or an ashtray. Your hands may occasionally be useful to emphasize a point; do not let them become a point of distraction.

3) Do not wisecrack or make small talk

This is a serious situation, and your attitude should show that you consider it as such. Further, the time of the board is limited – they do not want to waste it, and neither should you.

4) Do not exaggerate your experience or abilities

In the first place, from information in the application or other interviews and sources, the board may know more about you than you think. Secondly, you probably will not get away with it. An experienced board is rather adept at spotting such a situation, so do not take the chance.

5) If you know a board member, do not make a point of it, yet do not hide it

Certainly you are not fooling him, and probably not the other members of the board. Do not try to take advantage of your acquaintanceship – it will probably do you little good.

6) Do not dominate the interview

Let the board do that. They will give you the clues – do not assume that you have to do all the talking. Realize that the board has a number of questions to ask you, and do not try to take up all the interview time by showing off your extensive knowledge of the answer to the first one.

7) Be attentive

You only have 20 minutes or so, and you should keep your attention at its sharpest throughout. When a member is addressing a problem or question to you, give him your undivided attention. Address your reply principally to him, but do not exclude the other board members.

8) Do not interrupt

A board member may be stating a problem for you to analyze. He will ask you a question when the time comes. Let him state the problem, and wait for the question.

9) Make sure you understand the question

Do not try to answer until you are sure what the question is. If it is not clear, restate it in your own words or ask the board member to clarify it for you. However, do not haggle about minor elements.

10) Reply promptly but not hastily

A common entry on oral board rating sheets is "candidate responded readily," or "candidate hesitated in replies." Respond as promptly and quickly as you can, but do not jump to a hasty, ill-considered answer.

11) Do not be peremptory in your answers

A brief answer is proper – but do not fire your answer back. That is a losing game from your point of view. The board member can probably ask questions much faster than you can answer them.

12) Do not try to create the answer you think the board member wants

He is interested in what kind of mind you have and how it works – not in playing games. Furthermore, he can usually spot this practice and will actually grade you down on it.

13) Do not switch sides in your reply merely to agree with a board member

Frequently, a member will take a contrary position merely to draw you out and to see if you are willing and able to defend your point of view. Do not start a debate, yet do not surrender a good position. If a position is worth taking, it is worth defending.

14) Do not be afraid to admit an error in judgment if you are shown to be wrong

The board knows that you are forced to reply without any opportunity for careful consideration. Your answer may be demonstrably wrong. If so, admit it and get on with the interview.

15) Do not dwell at length on your present job

The opening question may relate to your present assignment. Answer the question but do not go into an extended discussion. You are being examined for a *new* job, not your present one. As a matter of fact, try to phrase ALL your answers in terms of the job for which you are being examined.

Basis of Rating

Probably you will forget most of these "do's" and "don'ts" when you walk into the oral interview room. Even remembering them all will not ensure you a passing grade. Perhaps you did not have the qualifications in the first place. But remembering them will help you to put your best foot forward, without treading on the toes of the board members.

Rumor and popular opinion to the contrary notwithstanding, an oral board wants you to make the best appearance possible. They know you are under pressure – but they also want to see how you respond to it as a guide to what your reaction would be under the pressures of the job you seek. They will be influenced by the degree of poise you display, the personal traits you show and the manner in which you respond.

ABOUT THIS BOOK

This book contains tests divided into Examination Sections. Go through each test, answering every question in the margin. At the end of each test look at the answer key and check your answers. On the ones you got wrong, look at the right answer choice and learn. Do not fill in the answers first. Do not memorize the questions and answers, but understand the answer and principles involved. On your test, the questions will likely be different from the samples. Questions are changed and new ones added. If you understand these past questions you should have success with any changes that arise. Tests may consist of several types of questions. We have additional books on each subject should more study be advisable or necessary for you. Finally, the more you study, the better prepared you will be. This book is intended to be the last thing you study before you walk into the examination room. Prior study of relevant texts is also recommended. NLC publishes some of these in our Fundamental Series. Knowledge and good sense are important factors in passing your exam. Good luck also helps. So now study this Passbook, absorb the material contained within and take that knowledge into the examination. Then do your best to pass that exam.

———

EXAMINATION SECTION

EXAMINATION SECTION
TEST 1

DIRECTIONS: Each question or incomplete statement is followed by several suggested
answers or completions. Select the one that BEST answers the question
or completes the statement. *PRINT THE LETTER OF THE CORRECT
ANSWER IN THE SPACE AT THE RIGHT.*

1. The transmission of signals by electromagnetic waves is referred to as   1._____

   A. biotelemetry   B. radio
   C. noise   D. all of the above

2. The transmission of physiologic data, such as an ECG, from the patient to a   2._____
   distant point of reception is called

   A. biotelemetry   B. simplex
   C. landline   D. none of the above

3. The assembly of a transmitter, receiver, and antenna connection at a fixed   3._____
   location creates a

   A. transceiver   B. radio
   C. biotelemetry   D. base station

4. The portion of the radio frequency spectrum between 30 and 150 mhz is called   4._____

   A. very high frequency (VHF)   B. ultrahigh frequency (UHF)
   C. very low frequency (VLF)   D. all of the above

5. A _____ is a miniature transmitter that picks up a radio signal and rebroad- 5._____
   casts it, thus extending the range of a radiocommunication system.

   A. transceiver   B. repeater   C. simplex   D. duplex

6. The portion of the radio frequency spectrum falling between 300 and 3,000   6._____
   mhz is called

   A. ultrahigh frequency (UHF)   B. very high frequency (VHF)
   C. very low frequency (VLF)   D. none of the above

7. One cycle per second equals one _____ in units of frequency.   7._____

   A. hertz   B. kilohertz   C. megahertz   D. gigahertz

8. The sources of noise in ECG telemetry include   8._____

   A. loose ECG electrodes
   B. muscle tremors
   C. sources of 60-cycle alternating current such as transformers, power lines,
      and electric equipment
   D. all of the above

9. The method of radio communications called _____ utilizes a single frequency that enables either transmission or reception of either voice or an ECG signal, but is incapable of simultaneous transmission and reception.

    A. duplex   B. simplex
    C. multiplex   D. none of the above

9.____

10. A terminal that receives transmissions of telemetry and voice from the field and transmits messages back through the base is referred to as a

    A. transceiver   B. remote control
    C. remote console   D. ten-code

10.____

11. The role of dispatcher includes

    A. reception of requests for help
    B. arrangements for getting the appropriate people and equipment to a situation which requires them
    C. deciding upon and dispatching of the appropriate emergency vehicles
    D. all of the above

11.____

12. A dispatcher should NOT

    A. maintain records
    B. scope a problem by requesting additional information from a caller
    C. direct public safety personnel
    D. receive notification of emergencies and call for assistance from both individual citizens and public safety units

12.____

13. The professional society of public safety communicators has developed a standard set of ten codes, the MOST common of which is 10-

    A. 1   B. 4   C. 12   D. 18

13.____

14. What is the meaning of 10-33?

    A. Help me quick   B. Arrived at scene
    C. Reply to message   D. Disregard

14.____

15. One of the MAIN purposes of ten-codes is to

    A. shorten air time
    B. complicate the message
    C. increase the likelihood of misunderstanding
    D. none of the above

15.____

Questions 16-20.

DIRECTIONS: In Questions 16 through 20, match each translation of a commonly
used ten-code with its appropriate code, listed in Column I.

<u>COLUMN I</u>

16.	What is your location?	A. 10-1	16._____
17.	Urgent.	B. 10-9	17._____
18.	Signal weak.	C. 10-18	18._____
19.	Arrived at the scene.	D. 10-20	19._____
20.	Please repeat.	E. 10-23	20._____

KEY (CORRECT ANSWERS)

1.	B		11.	D
2.	A		12.	C
3.	D		13.	B
4.	A		14.	A
5.	B		15.	A
6.	D		16.	D
7.	A		17.	C
8.	D		18.	A
9.	B		19.	E
10.	C		20.	B

TEST 2

DIRECTIONS: Each question or incomplete statement is followed by several suggested answers or completions. Select the one that BEST answers the question or completes the statement. *PRINT THE LETTER OF THE CORRECT ANSWER IN THE SPACE AT THE RIGHT.*

1. FCC rules prohibit

   A. deceptive or unnecessary messages
   B. profanity
   C. dissemination or use of confidential information transmitted over the radio
   D. all of the above

   1._____

2. Penalties for violations of FCC rules and regulations range from

   A. prison to death
   B. $20,000 to $100,000
   C. $100 to $10,000 and up to one year in prison
   D. up to 10 years in prison

   2._____

3. Which of the following is NOT true about base stations?

   A. The terrain and location do not affect the function.
   B. A good high-gain antenna improves transmission and reception efficiency.
   C. Multiple frequency capability is available at the base station.
   D. Antenna should be as close as possible to the base station transmitter/receiver.

   3._____

4. Radio frequencies are designated by cycles per second. 1,000,000 cycles per second equals one

   A. kilohertz   B. megahertz   C. gigahertz   D. hertz

   4._____

5. The Federal Communications Commission (FCC) is the agency of the United States government responsible for

   A. licensing and frequency allocation
   B. establishing technical standards for radio equipment
   C. establishing and enforcing rules and regulations for the operation of radio equipment
   D. all of the above

   5._____

6. Information relayed to the physician should include all of the following EXCEPT

   A. patient's age, sex, and chief complaint
   B. pertinent history of present illness
   C. detailed family history
   D. pertinent physical findings

   6._____

7. True statements regarding UHF band may include all of the following EXCEPT: 7._____

    A. It has better penetration in the dense metropolitan area
    B. Reception is usually quiet inside the building
    C. It has a longer range than VHF band
    D. Most medical communications occur around 450 to 470 mhz

8. Which of the following statements is NOT true regarding VHF band?   8._____

    A. Low band frequency may have ranges up to 2000 miles, but are unpredictable.
    B. VHF band may cause *skip interference*, with patchy losses in communication.
    C. High band frequency is wholly free of skip interference.
    D. High band frequencies for emergency medical purposes are in the 300 to 3000 mhz range.

9. 1000 cycles per second is equal to one   9._____

    A. hertz   B. kilohertz   C. megahertz   D. gigahertz

10. _____ achieves simultaneous transmission of voice and ECG signals over a single radio frequency.   10._____

    A. Duplex   B. Multiplex
    C. Channel   D. None of the above

11. Radio equipment used for both VHF and UHF band is   11._____

    A. frequency modulated
    B. amplitude modulated
    C. double amplitude modulated
    D. all of the above

12. ECG telemetry over UHF frequencies is confined to _____ of a 12 lead ECG.   12._____

    A. 1   B. 2   C. 6   D. 12

13. All of the following further clarity and conciseness EXCEPT   13._____

    A. understandable rate of speaking
    B. knowing what you want to transmit after transmission
    C. clear presentation of numbers, names, and dates
    D. using phrases and words which are easy to copy

14. The LEAST preferred of the following words is   14._____

    A. check   B. desire   C. want   D. advise if

15. All of the following are techniques useful during a call EXCEPT   15._____

    A. answering promptly
    B. identifying yourself and your department
    C. speaking directly into the mouthpiece
    D. none of the above

5

Questions 16-20.

DIRECTIONS: In Questions 16 through 20, match each definition with the term it describes, listed in Column I.

COLUMN I
A. Frequency
B. Noise
C. Patch
D. Duplex
E. Transceiver

16. A radio transmitter and receiver housed in a single unit; a two-way radio   16.____

17. The number of cycles per second of a radio signal, inversely related to the wavelength.   17.____

18. Interference in radio signals.   18.____

19. A radio system employing more than one frequency to permit simultaneous transmission and reception.   19.____

20. Connection between a telephone line and a radio communication system, enabling a caller to get *on the air* by special telephone.   20.____

KEY (CORRECT ANSWERS)

1.	D		11.	A
2.	C		12.	A
3.	A		13.	B
4.	B		14.	C
5.	D		15.	D
6.	C		16.	E
7.	C		17.	A
8.	D		18.	B
9.	B		19.	D
10.	B		20.	C

EXAMINATION SECTION
TEST 1

DIRECTIONS: Each question or incomplete statement is followed by several suggested answers or completions. Select the one that BEST answers the question or completes the statement. *PRINT THE LETTER OF THE CORRECT ANSWER IN TEE SPACE AT THE RIGHT.*

1. Police Communications Technicians must connect the caller to Transit Police when an incident occurs on a subway train or in the subway station.
   Which one of the following calls should be reported to Transit Police?

   A. The newsstand outside the entrance to the 86th Street subway was just robbed, and the suspects fled down the street.
   B. Soon after James Pike left the Columbus Circle subway station, his chain was snatched on the street corner.
   C. While traveling to work on the *D* line subway train, John Smith was mugged.
   D. A noisy group of school children have just come out of the Times Square subway station and are now annoying passersby on the street.

1.____

Question 2.

DIRECTIONS: Question 2 is to be answered SOLELY on the basis of the following information.
   When a Police Communications Technician is notified by patrol cars that they are in a vehicular pursuit, the dispatcher should obtain the following in the order given:

   I. Location of pursuit
   II. Type of vehicle, color of vehicle, and direction of travel
   III. Nature of offense
   IV. License plate number and state
   V. Number of occupant(s) in vehicle
   VI. Identity of the patrol car in pursuit

2. Police Communications Dispatcher Johnson is working the 26th Division when an unknown patrol car announces via car radio that he is in pursuit of a white 1986 Cadillac traveling north on Vanbrunt Street from Ainsley Place. Dispatcher Johnson then asks the pursuing patrol car, *What is the car wanted for?* The Officer replies, *The car is wanted for a hit and run.*
   What information should Dispatcher Johnson obtain NEXT?

   A. The number of occupant(s) in the vehicle
   B. Location of pursuit
   C. License plate number and state
   D. Identity of the patrol car in pursuit

2.____

Question 3.

DIRECTIONS: Question 3 is to be answered SOLELY on the basis of the following information.
Robbery - involves the unlawful taking of property from a person by force or attempted use of immediate force.

<u>Robbery in Progress</u> - crime is occurring at the time the call came into 911, 5 minutes in the past or when suspects are still in the area.

3. Which of the following situations would be considered a ROBBERY IN PROGRESS?   3._____

    A. Female calls 911 stating that she has just arrived home and found her apartment has been robbed.
    B. Male calls 911 stating that he just discovered that someone picked his pocket.
    C. Female calls 911 stating that she saw a man grab an elderly woman's purse.
    D. Child calls 911 stating that some man is beating up his mother and is trying to take her purse.

4. On June 20, 2007 at 6:30 P.M., Police Communications Technician White receives a call   4._____
from an anonymous complainant stating the following facts:

Incident:	Male with a gun sitting in a blue car
Location of Incident:	In front of 185 Hall St.
Description of Suspect:	Male, Black, bald, approximately 25 years old, dressed in red

Dispatcher White needs to be accurate and clear when transferring above information to the police dispatcher. Which one of the following expresses the above information MOST clearly and accurately?

    A. On June 20, 2007 at 6:30 P.M., a call was received stating that a bald man, dressed in red, was in front of 185 Hall St. A black male, approximately 25 years old, is sitting in a blue car holding a gun.
    B. A call was received on June 20, 2007. at 6:30 P.M. stating that a bald black male, approximately 25 years old, who is dressed in red, is armed with a gun sitting in a blue car in front of 185 Hall St.
    C. A call was received on June 20, 2007 at 6:30 P.M. Sitting in a blue car in front of 185 Hall St. is a Black male, approximately 25 years old. Dressed in red with a bald head, a man is armed with a gun.
    D. A call was received stating that in front of 185 Hall St., a bald male, approximately 25 years old, dressed in red, is sitting in a blue car. A Black male is armed with a gun at 6:30 P.M. on June 20, 2007.

5. Police Communications Technician Dozier receives a call from a female who has just wit-   5._____
nessed the following:

Incident:	White female police officer being assaulted
Location of Incident:	Surf Avenue and West 30th Street, in front of a candy store
Description of Suspectp;	Hispanic female wearing a green dress, possibly armed with a gun

Dispatcher Dozier is about to relay the information to the dispatcher.
Which one of the following expresses the above information MOST clearly and accurately?

    A. A call was received from a female on Surf Avenue and West 30th Street stating that a white female police officer is being assaulted by a Hispanic female wearing a green dress. She is possibly armed with a gun in front of a candy store.
    B. In front of a candy store at Surf Avenue and West 30th Street, a call was received from a female stating that a white female police officer is being assaulted by a Hispanic female wearing a green dress. She is possibly armed with a gun.

C. A call was received from a female stating that at the corner of Surf Avenue and West 30th Street in front of a candy store, there is a white female police officer being assaulted. The suspect is a Hispanic female wearing a green dress, who is possibly armed with a gun.

D. A call was received from a female stating that at the corner of West 30th Street and Surf Avenue, there is a white female police officer in front of a candy store being assaulted. She is wearing a green dress. The Hispanic female is possibly armed with a gun.

Questions 6-8.

DIRECTIONS: Questions 6 through 8 are to be answered SOLELY on the basis of the following passage.

At 10:35 A.M., Police Communications Technician Ross receives a second call from Mrs. Smith who is very upset because she has been waiting for the police and an ambulance since her first call, one hour ago. Mrs. Smith was mugged, and in resisting the attack, her nose was broken. The location of the incident is the uptown side of the subway station for the IND #2 train located at Jay Street and Borough Hall. Operator Ross advises Mrs. Smith to hold on and that she will check the status of her complaint. Operator Ross calls the Emergency Medical Service (EMS) and connects Mrs. Smith to the EMS operator. The EMS operator informs Mrs. Smith that an ambulance is coming from a far distance away and will be at the location at approximately 11:03 A.M. Operator Ross then calls the Transit Authority Police Department (TAPD). The TAPD received Mrs. Smith's first call at 9:37 A.M., and police arrived at location at 9:46 M. However, the police arrived at the downtown side of the subway station for the IND #3 train. TAPD informs Operator Ross that a police car will arrive at the correct location as soon as possible.

6. What is the CLOSEST approximate time that Mrs. Smith made her first call for help? _____ A.M.   6._____

    A. 9:35   B. 9:46   C. 10:35   D. 11:03 .

7. The ambulance was delayed because   7._____

    A. the ambulance responded to the downtown side of the subway station for the IND #2 train
    B. EMS never received Mrs. Smith's request for an ambulance
    C. a broken nose is not a priority request for an ambulance
    D. the ambulance was coming from a far distance

8. There was a delay in TAPD response to the crime scene because TAPD   8._____

    A. was coming from a far distance
    B. responded on the uptown side of the subway station for the IND #2 train
    C. was waiting for the -Police Department to respond first
    D. responded on the downtown side of the subway station for the IND #3 train

9. Extreme care must be taken when assigning solo cars (one police officer in a vehicle) to incidents. If anything in the job indicates that the job may be a potentially violent situation, a solo car should not be assigned.
In which one of the following incidents should a Police Communications Technician assign a solo car?
A

   A. disorderly male carrying a knife
   B. house that was broken into two days ago
   C. suspiciously occupied auto
   D. group of rowdy teenagers throwing beer bottles at passersbys

9.____

Question 10.

DIRECTIONS: Question 10 is to be answered SOLELY on the basis of the following information.

On the Police Communications Technician's screen, the following incidents appear which were called in at the same time:

   I. Caller states that she is looking out her 10th floor window and sees a man sleeping on the street in front of her home at Crescent Street and 4th Avenue.
   II. Caller states that he was driving down the block of Crescent Street between 3rd and 4th Avenues and just witnessed a man being beaten and mugged. The caller thinks that the victim is unconscious.
   III. Caller states there is a car accident at Crescent Street and 3rd Avenue, and one of the passengers suffered a broken arm.

10. Which of the above should the operator MOST likely consider as the same incident?

   A. I and II
   C. I and III
   B. II and III
   D. I, II, and III

10.____

11. Police Communications Operator Raymond receives a call regarding a rape and obtains the following information:

Time of Rape: 10:35 P.M.
Place of Rape: Sam's Laundromat, 200 Melrose Avenue
Victim: Joan McGraw
Crime: Rape
Suspect: Male, Hispanic, carrying a gun

Operator Raymond is about to enter the incident into the computer.
Which one of the following expresses the above information MOST clearly and accurately?

   A. At 10:35 P.M., Joan McGraw was raped in Sam's Laundromat, located at 200 Melrose Avenue, by a Hispanic male carrying a gun.
   B. A Hispanic male was carrying a gun at 10:35 P.M. Joan McGraw was raped in Sam's Laundromat located at 200 Melrose Avenue.
   C. Carrying a gun, Joan McGraw was raped by a Hispanic male. This occurred in Sam's Laundromat located at 200 Melrose Avenue at 10:35 P.M.
   D. At 10:35 P.M., Joan McGraw was raped by a Hispanic male carrying a gun. Sam's Laundromat is located at 200 Melrose Avenue.

11.____

12. Police Communications Dispatcher Gold receives a call concerning a disorderly male in a local drug store. He obtains the following information:

Place of Occurrence: Rapid-Serve Drug Store
Complainant: George Meyer
Crime: Threatening gestures and abusive language
Suspect: Male, white
Action Taken: The suspect was removed from premises by the police.

Dispatcher Gold is about to enter the incident into the computer.
Which one of the following expresses the above information MOST clearly and accurately?

12.____

    A. George Meyer called the police because a white male was removed from the Rapid-Serve Drug Store. He was making threatening gestures and using abusive language.
    B. George Meyer called the police and was removed from the Rapid-Serve Drug Store. A white male was making threatening gestures and using abusive language.
    C. At the Rapid-Serve Drug Store, a white male was making threatening gestures and using abusive language. George Meyer called the police and removed the suspect from the drug store.
    D. George Meyer called the police because a white male was making threatening gestures and using abusive language in the Rapid-Serve Drug Store. The suspect was removed from the drug store by the police.

Question 13.

DIRECTIONS: Question 13 is to be answered SOLELY on the basis of the following information.

When dispatching an incident involving a suspicious package, a Police Communications Technician should do the following in the order given:

    I. Assign a patrol car and Patrol Sergeant.
    II. Enter into the computer additional information received from assigned cars.
    III. Notify appropriate Emergency Assistance.
    IV. Notify the Bomb Squad.
    V. Notify the Duty Captain.

13. Police Communications Technician Berlin receives a call involving a suspicious package located on the corner of Gates Avenue and Blake Street. Dispatcher Berlin promptly assigns a patrol car and a Patrol Sergeant to the incident. Upon arrival, the Sergeant determines that there is a ticking sound coming from the box. The Sergeant immediately advises Dispatcher Berlin of the situation and tells Dispatcher Berlin to call the Fire Department and have them respond.
What should Dispatcher Berlin to NEXT?

13.____

    A. Call the Fire Department.
    B. Notify the Bomb Squad.
    C. Enter additional information received from assigned cars into the computer.
    D. Notify the Duty Captain.

Questions 14-16.

DIRECTIONS: Questions 14 through 16 are to be answered SOLELY on the basis of the following passage.

Police Communications Technician Robbins receives a call at 5:15 P.M. from Mr. Adams reporting he witnessed a shooting in front of 230 Eagle Road. Mr. Adams, who lives at 234 Eagle Road, states he overheard two white males arguing with a Black man. He describes one white male as having blonde hair and wearing a black jacket with blue jeans, and the other white male as having brown hair and wearing a white jacket and blue jeans.

Mr. Adams recognized the Black man as John Rivers, the son of Mrs. Mary Rivers, who lives at 232 Eagle Road. At 5:10 P.M., the blonde male took a gun, shot John in the stomach, and dragged his body into the alleyway. The two males ran into the backyard of 240 Eagle Road and headed west on Randall Boulevard. Dispatcher Robbins connects Mr. Adams to the Emergency Medical Service. The Ambulance Receiving Operator processes the call at 5:25 P.M. and advises Mr. Adams that the next available ambulance will be sent.

14.   Who was the eyewitness to the shooting?   14._____

    A.   Dispatcher Robbins   B.   Mr. Adams
    C.   Mrs. Rivers   D.   John Rivers

15.   In front of what address was John Rivers shot?   15._____
      _____ Eagle Road.

    A.   230   B.   232   C.   234   D.   240

16.   What is the description of the male who fired the gun? A male wearing a _____ jacket   16._____
      and blue jeans.

    A.   white blonde-haired; white
    B.   white brown-haired; black
    C.   white blonde-haired; black
    D.   Black brown-haired; white

17.   A Police Communications Technician can have several calls for police response on their   17._____
      computer screen at one time. A dispatcher may have to determine which of the calls is
      the most serious and assign that one to the police first.
      Which one of the following situations should a dispatcher assign to the police FIRST?

    A.   A robbery which occurred two hours ago, and the suspects have fled the scene
    B.   A suspicious man offering a child candy to get the child into his van at the time of
         the call
    C.   A woman returns to her car and finds her left fender dented
    D.   A group of youths playing cards in the hallway

18.   The following information was obtained by Police Communications Technician Fried   18._____
      regarding a call of an auto accident with injuries:
      Date of Accident: March 7, 2007
      Place of Accident: 50 West 96th Street
      Time of Accident: 3:15 P.M.
      Drivers: Susan Green and Nancy White

Injured: Nancy White
Action Taken: Emergency Medical Services (EMS) Operator 600 was notifed
Dispatcher Fried is about to enter the above information into the computer.
Which one of the following expresses the above information MOST clearly and accurately?

- A. At 50 West 96th Street, Susan Green and Nancy White had an auto accident resulting in an injury to Nancy White. EMS Operator 600 was notifed to send an ambulance at 3:15 P.M. on March 7, 2007.
- B. EMS Operator 600 was notified to send an ambulance to 50 West 96th Street due to an auto accident between Nancy White and Susan Green, who was injured on March 7, 2007 at 3:15 P.M.
- C. Susan Green and Nancy White were involved in an auto accident at 50 West 96th Street on March 7, 2007. At 3:15 P.M., EMS Operator 600 was notified to send an ambulance for Nancy White.
- D. On March 7, 2007 at 3:15 P.M., Susan Green and Nancy White were involved in an auto accident at 50 West 96th Street. EMS Operator 600 was notified to send an ambulance for Nancy White who was injured in the accident.

Questions 19-20.

DIRECTIONS: Questions 19 and 20 are to be answered SOLELY on the basis of the following information.

At the beginning of their tours, Police Communications Technicians need to call the precinct to find out what patrol cars are covering which sections of the precinct and which special assignment cars are being used. Special assignment cars are used instead of regular patrol cars when certain situations arise. Special assignment cars should be assigned before a patrol car when a call comes in that is related to the car's special assignment, regardless of what section the incident is occurring in. Otherwise, a regular patrol car should be assigned.

Police Communications Technician Tanner is assigned to the 83rd Precinct. He calls the precinct and determines the following patrol cars and special assignment cars are being used:

Patrol cars are assigned as follows:
  Patrol Car 83A - Covers Sections A, B, C
  Patrol Car 83D - Covers Sections D, E, F
  Patrol Car 83G - Covers Sections G, H, I

Special assignment cars are assigned as follows:
  83SP1 - Burglary Car
  83SP2 - Religious Establishment
  83SP8 - Anti-Crime (plainclothes officers)

19. Dispatcher Tanner receives a call located in the 83rd Precinct in *E* Section. Which car should be assigned?   19.____

   A. 83D   B. 83A   C. 83SP8   D. 83SP2

20. Dispatcher Tanner receives a call concerning a burglary in *B* Section. Which is the CORRECT car to be assigned?   20.____

   A. 83A   B. 83G   C. 83SP1   D. 83SP2

13

KEY (CORRECT ANSWERS)

1.	C	11.	A
2.	C	12.	D
3.	D	13.	C
4.	B	14.	B
5.	C	15.	A
6.	A	16.	C
7.	D	17.	B
8.	D	18.	D
9.	B	19.	A
10.	A	20.	C

———

TEST 2

DIRECTIONS: Each question or incomplete statement is followed by several suggested answers or completions. Select the one that BEST answers the question or completes the statement. *PRINT THE LETTER OF THE CORRECT ANSWER IN THE SPACE AT THE RIGHT.*

1. Police Communications Technician Daniel receives a call stating the following: 1.____

   Date and Time of Call: June 21, 2007 at 12:30 P.M.
Incident:	Shots being fired
Location:	The roof of a building, located between Moore Street and Bushwick Avenue, exact address unknown
Suspect:	Male
Complainant:	Mr. Bernard
Comments:	Mr. Bernard will be wearing a brown coat and will direct officers to location of the incident.

   Dispatcher Daniel is about to enter the information into the computer.
   Which one of the following expresses the above information MOST clearly and accurately?
   On June 21, 2007,

   A. at 12:30 P.M., Dispatcher Daniel receives a call from a complainant stating that a male is on a roof of a building with an unknown address firing a gun, and he is wearing a brown coat. The complainant, Mr. Bernard, will be in front of the building to direct the police to the exact location of the incident.
   B. a male is firing a gun from a roof, stated complainant Mr. Bernard to Dispatcher Daniel. This is at Moore Street and Bushwick Avenue. At 12:30 P.M., the caller will be at the location to direct the police to the building where the male is firing the gun. He is wearing a brown coat.
   C. at 12:30 P.M., Dispatcher Daniel receives a call from a complainant, Mr. Bernard, who states that at a building with an unknown address, located between Moore Street and Bushwick Avenue, a male is firing a gun from a roof. Mr. Bernard will be at the location wearing a brown coat to direct the police to the exact building.
   D. Dispatcher Daniel receives a call from a complainant, Mr. Bernard, who is calling from a building with an unknown address. He informs Dispatcher Daniel that a male is firing a gun from a roof of a building between Moore Street and Bushwick Avenue. At 12:30 P.M., Mr. Bernard will be wearing a brown coat to direct the police to the incident.

Questions 2-4.

DIRECTIONS: Questions 2 through 4 are to be answered SOLELY on the basis of the following passage.

Mrs. Arroyo returns from work one evening to find her door open and loud noise coming from her apartment. She peeks through the crack of the door and sees a white male moving rapidly through her apartment wearing blue jeans and a pink T-shirt. She runs to the nearest public telephone and dials 911. Police Communications Technician Ms. Lopez takes the call. Mrs. Arroyo informs Operator Lopez that there is a strange man in her apartment. The operator asks the caller for her address, apartment number, name, and telephone number, and then puts Mrs. Arroyo on hold. Operator Lopez enters the address in the computer and, realizing it is a high priority call, tries to notify the Radio Dispatcher directly by depressing the *hotline* button.

The Radio Dispatcher does not respond, and Operator Lopez realizes the *hotline* button is not working. The operator then continues to enter the rest of the information into the computer and notifies the caller that the police will respond. Operator Lopez then walks into the dispatcher's room to make sure the dispatcher received the information entered into the computer, and then notifies the supervisor of her malfunctioning equipment.

2. The operator notified her supervisor because   2.____

    A. the suspect was still in the apartment
    B. the *hotline* button was not working
    C. she could not enter the address in the computer
    D. it was a high priority call

3. What was the FIRST action the operator took after putting the complainant on hold?   3.____

    A. Entered the caller's telephone number and name in the computer.
    B. Walked into the dispatcher's room.
    C. Entered the caller's address into the computer.
    D. Tried to notify the Radio Dispatcher by depressing the *hotline* button.

4. Operator Lopez depressed the *hotline* button   4.____

    A. to check if the *hotline* button was working properly
    B. because it was a high priority call
    C. to make sure the dispatcher received the information entered into the computer
    D. because the computer was not working properly

Question 5.

DIRECTIONS: Question 5 is to be answered SOLELY on the basis of the following information.

A Police Communications Technician occasionally receives calls from persons making threats against public officials, visiting dignitaries, or members of the Police Department. When this occurs, the Dispatcher should do the following in the order given:

    I. Obtain details of the threat
        (A) Who is being threatened and how
        (B) When it is going to happen
    II. Attempt to determine the sex and ethnicity of the caller
    III. Try to obtain the identity, address, and telephone number of the caller
    IV. Notify the supervisor

5. Police Communications Operator Frye receives a call and obtains from the caller that he is going to shoot the mayor on Election Day. Operator Frye determine the caller to be a male with a heavy Hispanic accent. Operator Frye asks the male for his name, address, and phone number. The caller does not respond and hangs up.   5.____
What should Operator Frye do NEXT?

    A. Obtain details of the threats.
    B. Determine the sex and ethnicity of the caller.
    C. Obtain the identity, address, and phone number of the caller.
    D. Notify the supervisor.

Question 6.

DIRECTIONS: Question 6 is to be answered SOLELY on the basis of the following informa-
            tion.

A Police Communications Technician will call back complainants only under the following
conditions:
   1.   Dispatcher needs clarification of information previously received from the com-
        plainant and/or
   2.   To notify the complainant that police need to gain entry to the location of the inci-
        dent.

6.   In which one of the following situations should a Police Communications Technician call   6._____
     back the complainant?

     A.   While responding to an assigned incident, Patrol Car 79A gets a flat tire. Patrol Car
          79A radios the dispatcher and advises the dispatcher to call the complainant and
          notify the complainant that there will be a delay in police response.
     B.   Patrol Car 83B is assigned to an incident that occurred approximately 30 minutes
          ago. Patrol Car 83B advises the dispatcher that he is coming from a far distance
          and the dispatcher should call the complainant to find out which is the best way to
          get to the incident location.
     C.   Patrol Car 66B is on the scene of an incident and is having a problem gaining entry
          into the building. Patrol Car 66B asks the dispatcher to call the complainant and
          ask him to meet the police officers from the patrol car outside the building.
     D.   Patrol Car 90B is assigned to a burglary that occurred in the complainant's private
          home. It is raining heavily outside, so Patrol Car 90B asks the dispatcher to call
          and request the complainant to meet the police by the patrol car.

7.   Police Communications Dispatcher Blake receives a call reporting a bank robbery and   7._____
     obtains the following information:

     Time of Robbery: 11:30 A.M.
     Place of Robbery: Fidelity Bank
     Crime: Bank Robbery
     Suspect: Male, white, wearing blue jeans, blue jacket, carrying a brown
                             bag
     Witness: Susan Lane of 731 Madison Avenue

     Dispatcher Blake is about to inform his supervisor of the facts concerning the bank
     robbery.
     Which one of the following expresses the above information MOST clearly and accu-
     rately?

     A.   At 11:30 A.M., the Fidelity Bank was robbed. Susan Lane lives at 731 Madison
          Avenue. The witness saw a white male wearing blue jeans, a blue jacket, and car-
          rying a brown bag.
     B.   Susan Lane of 731 Madison Avenue witnessed the robbery of Fidelity Bank at
          11:30 A.M. The suspect is a white male and was wearing blue jeans, a blue jacket,
          and carrying a brown bag.
     C.   Wearing blue jeans, a blue jacket, and carrying a brown bag, Susan Lane of 731
          Madison Avenue saw a white male robbing the Fidelity Bank. The robbery was wit-
          nessed at 11:30 A.M.

D.   At 11:30 A.M., Susan Lane of 731 Madison Avenue witnessed the robbery of the Fidelity Bank. A white male wore blue jeans, a blue jacket, and carried a brown bag.

8.   Police Communications Technician Levine receives an incident for dispatch containing the following information:

Incident:	A female being beaten
Location:	In front of 385 Wall Street
Victim:	White female
Suspect:	White, male, wearing a grey shirt, possibly concealing a gun underneath his shirt

Dispatcher Levine is about to relay this information to the patrol car.
Which one of the following expresses the above information MOST clearly and accurately?

   A.   A white female is being beaten by a white male wearing a grey shirt, who is possibly concealing a gun underneath his shirt. This is occurring in front of 385 Wall Street.
   B.   A white male is beating a white female wearing a grey shirt. He is possibly concealing a gun underneath his shirt in front of 385 Wall Street.
   C.   A female is being beaten in front of 385 Wall Street. A white male is possibly concealing a gun underneath his shirt. She is white, and the suspect is wearing a grey shirt.
   D.   In front of 385 Wall Street, a white female is being beaten by a suspect, possibly concealing a gun underneath his shirt. A white male is wearing a grey shirt.

8.____

Questions 9-11.

DIRECTIONS: Questions 9 through 11 are to be answered SOLELY on the basis of the following passage.

Police Communications Technician John Clove receives a call from a Social Worker, Mrs. Norma Harris of Presbyterian Hospital, who states there is a 16-year-old teenager on the other line, speaking to Dr. Samuel Johnson, a psychologist at the hospital. The teenager is threatening suicide and claims that she is an out-patient, but refuses to give her name, address, or telephone number. She further states that the teenager took 100 pills of valium and is experiencing dizziness, numbness of the lips, and heart palpitations. The teenager tells Dr. Johnson that she wants to die because her boyfriend left her because she is pregnant.

Dr. Johnson is keeping her on the line persuading her to give her name, telephone number, and address. The Social Worker asks the dispatcher to trace the call. The dispatcher puts the caller on hold and informs his supervisor, Mrs. Ross, of the incident. The supervisor contacts Telephone Technician Mr. Ralph Taylor. Mr. Taylor contacts the telephone company and speaks to Supervisor Wallace, asking him to trace the call between Dr. Johnson and the teenager. After approximately 10 minutes, the dispatcher gets back to the Social Worker and informs her that the call is being traced.

9.   Why did the Social Worker call Dispatcher Clove?

   A.   A teenager is threatening suicide.
   B.   Mrs. Ross took 100 pills of valium.

9.____

C. Dr. Johnson felt dizzy, numbness of the lips, and heart palpitations.
D. An unmarried teenager is pregnant.

10. Who did Mr. Clove notify FIRST?   10.____

    A. Mrs. Norma Harris   B. Dr. Samuel Johnson
    C. Mr. Wallace   D. Mrs. Ross

11. The conversation between which two individuals is being traced?   11.____

    A. Mrs. Norma Harris and the 16-year-old teenager
    B. The Telephone Technician and Telephone Company Supervisor
    C. Dr. Johnson and the 16-year-old teenager
    D. The dispatcher and the Hospital Social Worker

Question 12.

DIRECTIONS: Question 12 is to be answered SOLELY on the basis of the following information.

On the Police Communications Technician's screen, the following incidents appear which were called in at the same time by three different callers:

    I. A fight is occurring at 265 Hall Street between Myrtle and Willoughby Ave. The fight started in Apartment 3C, and the two men are now fighting in the street.
    II. A fight took place between a security guard and a suspected shoplifter in a store at Hall St. and Willoughby Ave. The security guard is holding the suspect in the security office.
    III. A fight is occurring between two white males on the street near the corner of Hall Street and Myrtle Ave. One of the males has a baseball bat.

12. Which of the above should a Police Communications Technician MOST likely consider as the same incident?   12.____

    A. I and II   B. II and III
    C. I and III   D. I, II, and III

Questions 13-15.

DIRECTIONS: Questions 13 through 15 are to be answered SOLELY on the basis of the following passage.

Police Communications Technician Flood receives a call from Mr. Michael Watkins, Program Director for *Meals on Wheels*, a program that delivers food to elderly people who cannot leave their home. Mr. Watkins states he received a call from Rochelle Berger, whose elderly aunt, Estelle Sims, is a client of his. Rochelle Berger informed Mr. Watkins that she has just received a call from her aunt's neighbor, Sally Bowles, who told her that her aunt has not eaten in several days and is in need of medical attention.

After questioning Mr. Watkins, Dispatcher Flood is informed that Estelle Sims lives at 300 79th Street in Apartment 6K, and her telephone number is 686-4527; Sally Bowles lives in Apartment 6H, and her telephone number is 678-2456. Mr. Watkins further advises that if there is difficulty getting into Estelle Sims' apartment, to ring Sally Bowies' bell and she will let you in. Mr. Watkins gives his phone number as 776-0451, and Rochelle Berger's phone number is 291-7287. Dispatcher Flood advises Mr. Watkins that the appropriate medical assistance will be sent.

13. Who did Sally Bowles notify that her neighbor needed medical attention?   13._____

    A. Dispatcher Flood   B. Michael Watkins
    C. Rochelle Berger   D. Estelle Sims

14. If the responding medical personnel are unable to get into Apartment 6K, they should   14._____
speak to

    A. Rochelle Berger   B. Sally Bowles
    C. Dispatcher Flood   D. Michael Watkins

15. Whose telephone number is 686-4527?   15._____

    A. Michael Watkins   B. Estelle Sims
    C. Sally Bowles   D. Rochelle Berger

16. Police Communications Technicians often receive calls regarding incidents where a   16._____
response from the Fire Department may be necessary.
In which one of the following situations would a request from the dispatcher for the Fire
Department to respond be MOST critical?
A(n)

    A. fire hydrant has been opened by children on a hot August afternoon
    B. abandoned auto is parked in front of a fire hydrant
    C. neighbor's cat has climbed up a tree and is stuck
    D. excited woman smells smoke coming from the floor below

Question 17.

DIRECTIONS: Question 17 is to be answered SOLELY on the basis of the following informa-
                  tion.

When a patrol car confirms that a murder has taken place, the Police Communications
Technician should notify the following people in the order given:

     I. Patrol Sergeant
    II. Dispatching Supervisor
   III. Operations Unit
   IV. Crime Scene Unit
    V. Precinct Detective Unit
   VI. Duty Captain

17. Police Communications Technician Rodger assigns a patrol car to investigate a man who   17._____
was shot and killed. The patrol car arrives on the scene and confirms that a murder has
taken place. The Patrol Sergeant hears what has happened on his police radio and
informs Dispatcher Rodger that he is going to respond to the scene. The Dispatching
Supervisor walks over to Dispatcher Rodger and is informed of the situation.
Who should Dispatcher Rodger notify NEXT?

    A. Operations Unit   B. Patrol Sergeant
    C. Precinct Detective Unit   D. Crime Scene Unit

18. Police Communications Technician Peterson receives a call from a woman inside the subway station reporting that her purse has just been snatched. Dispatcher Peterson obtained the following information relating to the crime:

Place of Occurrence: E. 42nd Street and Times Square
Time of Occurrence: 5:00 P.M.
Crime: Purse Snatched
Victim: Thelma Johnson
Description of Suspect: Black, female, brown hair, blue jeans, red T-shirt
Dispatcher Peterson is about to relay the information to the Transit Authority Police Dispatcher.
Which one of the following expresses the above information MOST clearly and accurately?

   18.____

A. At 5:00 P.M., a brown-haired Black woman snatched a purse inside the subway station at E. 42nd Street and Times Square belonging to Thelma Johnson. She was wearing blue jeans and a red T-shirt.
B. A purse was snatched from Thelma Johnson by a woman with brown hair in the subway station at 5:00 P.M. A Black female was wearing blue jeans and a red T-shirt at E. 42nd Street and Times Square.
C. At 5:00 P.M., Thelma Johnson's purse was snatched inside the subway station at E. 42nd Street and Times Square. The suspect is a Black female with brown hair who is wearing blue jeans and a red T-shirt.
D. Thelma Johnson reported at 5:00 P.M. her purse was snatched. In the subway station at E. 42nd Street and Times Square, a Black female with brown hair was wearing blue jeans and a red T-shirt.

19. Police Communications Technician Hopkins receives a call of an assault and obtains the following information concerning the incident:

Place of Occurrence: Times Square
Time of Occurrence: 3:15 A.M.
Victim: Peter Polk
Victim's Address: 50 E. 60 Street
Suspect: Male, Hispanic, 5'6", 140 lbs., dressed in black
Injury: Broken nose
Action Taken: Victim transported to St. Luke's Hospital
Dispatcher Hopkins is about to enter the job into the computer system.
Which one of the following expresses the above information MOST clearly and accurately?

   19.____

A. At 3:15 A.M., Peter Polk was assaulted in Times Square by a Hispanic male, 5'6", 140 lbs., dressed in black, suffering a broken nose. Mr. Polk lives at 50 E. 69 Street and was transported to St. Luke's Hospital.
B. At 3:15 A.M., Peter Polk was assaulted in Times Square by a Hispanic male, 5'6", 140 lbs., dressed in black, who lives at 50 E. 69 Street. Mr. Polk suffered a broken nose and was transported to St. Luke's Hospital.
C. Peter Polk, who lives at 50 E. 69 Street, was assaulted at 3:15 A.M. in Times Square by a Hispanic male, 5'6", 140 lbs., dressed in black. Mr. Polk suffered a broken nose and was transported to St. Luke's Hospital.
D. Living at 50 E. 69 Street, Mr. Polk suffered a broken nose and was transported to St. Luke's Hospital. At 3:15 A.M., Mr. Polk was assaulted by a Hispanic male, 5'6", 140 lbs., who was dressed in black.

20. A Police Communications Technician is required to determine which situations called in   20.____
to 911 require police assistance and which calls require non-emergency assistance.
Which one of the following calls should a dispatcher MOST likely refer to non-emergency assistance?

    A. Mr. Moss threatens the owner of Deluxe Deli with bodily harm for giving him incor-
rect change of twenty dollars.

    B. The manager refuses to take back Mrs. Thompson's defective toaster because she
doesn't have a receipt. Mrs. Thompson leaves the store.

    C. Mrs. Frank is having a violent argument with the manager of Donna's Dress Shop
because he is refusing to exchange a dress she recently purchased.

    D. The manager of Metro Supermarket refuses to take back a stale loaf of bread, so
the consumer punches him in the face.

_____

KEY (CORRECT ANSWERS)

1.	C	11.	C
2.	B	12.	C
3.	C	13.	C
4.	B	14.	B
5.	D	15.	B
6.	C	16.	D
7.	B	17.	A
8.	A	18.	C
9.	A	19.	C
10.	D	20.	B

_____

22

EXAMINATION SECTION
TEST 1

DIRECTIONS: Each question or incomplete statement is followed by several suggested answers or completions. Select the one that BEST answers the question or completes the statement. *PRINT THE LETTER OF THE CORRECT ANSWER IN THE SPACE AT THE RIGHT.*

Questions 1-3.

DIRECTIONS: Questions 1 through 3 are to be answered SOLELY on the basis of the following passage.

On May 15 at 10:15 A.M., Mr. Price was returning to his home at 220 Kings Walk when he discovered two of his neighbor's apartment doors slightly opened. One neighbor, Mrs. Kagan, who lives alone in Apartment 1C, was away on vacation. The other apartment, IB, is occupied by Martin and Ruth Stone, an elderly couple, who usually take a walk everyday at 10:00 A.M. Fearing a robbery might be taking place, Mr. Price runs downstairs to Mr. White in Apartment BI to call the police. Police Communications Technician Johnson received the call at 10:20 A.M. Mr. Price gave his address and stated that two apartments were possibly being burglarized. Communications Technician Johnson verified the address in the computer and then asked Mr. Price for descriptions of the suspects. He explained that he had not seen anyone, but he believed that they were still inside the building. Communications Technician Johnson immediately notified the dispatcher who assigned two patrol cars at 10:25 A.M., while Mr. Price was still on the phone. Communications Technician Johnson told Mr. Price that the police were responding to the location.

1. Who called Communications Technician Johnson?   1.____

   A. Mrs. Kagan   B. Mr. White
   C. Mrs. Stone   D. Mr. Price

2. What time did Communications Technician Johnson receive the call?   2.____
   _____ A.M.

   A. 10:00   B. 10:15   C. 10:20   D. 10:25

3. Which tenant was away on vacation?   3.____
   The tenant in Apartment

   A. 1C   B. IB   C. BI   D. ID

4. Dispatcher Watkins receives the following information regarding a complaint.   4.____
   Place of occurrence: St. James Park
   Complaint: Large group of intoxicated males throwing beer bottles
                               and playing loud music
   Complainant: Oscar Aker
   Complainant's Address: 13 St. James Square, Apt. 2B
   Dispatcher Watkins is not certain if this incident should be reported to 911 or Mr. Aker's local precinct. Dispatcher Watkins is about to notify his supervisor of the call. Which one of the following expresses the above information MOST clearly and accurately?

A. Mr. Aker, who lives at 13 St. James Square, Apt. 2B, called to make a complaint of a large group of intoxicated males who are throwing beer bottles and playing loud music in St. James Park.
B. Mr. Aker, who lives at 13 St. James Square, called to complain about a large group of intoxicated males, in Apt. 2B. They are throwing beer bottles and playing loud music in St. James Park.
C. Mr. Aker of 13 St. James Square, Apt. 2B, called to complain about loud music. There were a large group of intoxicated males throwing beer bottles in St. James Park.
D. As a result of intoxicated males throwing beer bottles Mr. Aker of 13 St. James Square, Apt. 2B, called to complain. A large group was playing loud music in St. James Park.

5. Communications Operator Davis recorded the following information from a caller: 5._____
Crime: Rape
Time of Rape: 11:30 A.M.
Place of Rape: Ralph's Dress Shop, 200 Lexington
Avenue Victim: Linda Castro - employee at Ralph's Dress Shop
Description of Suspect: Male, white
Weapon: Knife
Communications Operator Davis needs to be clear and accurate when relaying information to the patrol car. Which one of the following expresses the above information MOST clearly and accurately?

A. Linda Castro was at 200 Lexington Avenue when she was raped at knife point by a white male. At 11:30 A.M., she is an employee of Ralph's Dress Shop.
B. At 11:30 A.M., Linda Castro reported that she was working in Ralph's Dress Shop located at 200 Lexington Avenue. A white male raped her while she was working at knife point.
C. Linda Castro, an employee of Ralph's Dress Shop, located at 200 Lexington Avenue, reported that at 11:30 A.M. a white male raped her at knife point in the dress shop.
D. At 11:30 A.M., a white male pointed a knife at Linda Castro. He raped an employee of Ralph's Dress Shop, which is located at 200 Lexington Avenue.

Question 6.

DIRECTIONS: Question 6 is to be answered SOLELY on the basis of the following information.

Police Communications Technicians frequently receive low priority calls, which are calls that do not require an immediate police response. When a low priority call is received, the Police Communications Technician should transfer the caller to a tape-recorded message which states *there will be a delay in police response.*

6. Police Communications Technicians should transfer to the low priority taped message a   6._____
call reporting a

A. hubcap missing from an auto
B. child has just swallowed poison

24

C. group of youths fighting with knives
D. woman being assaulted

Questions 7-9.

DIRECTIONS: Questions 7 through 9 are to be answered SOLELY on the basis of the following passage.

On Tuesday, March 20 at 11:55 P.M., Dispatcher Uzel receives a call from a female stating that she immediately needs the police. The dispatcher asks the caller for her address. The excited female answers, *I can not think of it right now.* The dispatcher tries to calm down the caller. At this point, the female caller tells the dispatcher that her address is 1934 Bedford Avenue. The caller then realizes that 1934 Bedford Avenue is her mother's address and gives her address as 3455 Bedford Avenue. Dispatcher Uzel enters the address into the computer and tells the caller that the cross streets are Myrtle and Willoughby Avenues. The caller answers, *I don't live near Willoughby Avenue.* The dispatcher repeats her address at 3455 Bedford Avenue. Then the female states that her name is Linda Harris and her correct address is 5534 Bedford Avenue. Dispatcher Uzel enters the new address into the computer and determines the cross streets to be Utica Avenue and Kings Highway. The caller agrees that these are the cross streets where she lives.

7. What is the caller's CORRECT address?   7.____

    A. Unknown   B. 1934 Bedford Avenue
    C. 3455 Bedford Avenue   D. 5534 Bedford Avenue

8. What are the cross streets of the correct address?   8.____

    A. Myrtle Avenue and Willoughby Avenue
    B. Utica Avenue and Kings Highway
    C. Bedford Avenue and Myrtle Avenue
    D. Utica Avenue and Willoughby Avenue

9. Why did the female caller telephone Dispatcher Uzel?   9.____

    A. She needed the cross streets for her address.
    B. Her mother needed assistance.
    C. The purpose of the call was not mentioned.
    D. She did not know where she lived.

Question 10.

DIRECTIONS: Question 10 is to be answered SOLELY on the basis of the following information.

When performing vehicle license plate checks, Operators should do the following in the order given:

    I. Request the license plate in question.
    II. Repeat the license plate back to the patrol car officers.
    III. Check the license plate locally in the computer.
    IV. Advise the patrol car officers of the results of the local check.
    V. Check the license plate nationally in the computer.
    VI. Advise the patrol car officers of the results of the nationwide check.

10. Operator Johnson gets a request from a patrol car officer for a license plate check on a suspicious car. The patrol car officer tells Operator Johnson that the license plate number is XYZ-843, which Operator Johnson repeats back to the patrol car officer. Operator Johnson checks the license plate locally and determines that the car was stolen in the New York City area.
What should Operator Johnson do NEXT?

    A. Repeat the license plate back to patrol car officers.
    B. Check the license plate nationally.
    C. Advise the patrol car officers of the results of the local check.
    D. Advise the patrol ear officers of the results of the nationwide check.

10.____

11. Police Communications Technician Hughes receives a call from the owner of The Diamond Dome Jewelry Store, reporting a robbery. He obtains the following information from the caller:

Place of Occurrence: The Diamond Dome Jewelry Store, 10 Exchange Place
Time of Occurrence: 10:00 A.M.
Crime: Robbery of a $50,000 diamond ring
Victim: Clayton Pelt, owner of The Diamond Dome Jewelry Store
Description of Suspect: Male, white, black hair, blue suit and gray shirt
Weapon: Gun

Communications Technician Hughes is about to relay the information to the dispatcher. Which one of the following expresses the above information MOST clearly and accurately?

    A. Clayton Pelt reported that at 10:00 A.M. his store, The Diamond Dome Jewelry Store, was robbed at gunpoint. At 10 Exchange Place, a white male with black hair took a $50,000 diamond ring. He was wearing a blue suit and gray shirt.
    B. At 10:00 A.M., a black-haired male robbed a $50,000 diamond ring from The Diamond Dome Jewelry Store, which is owned by Clayton Pelt. A white male was wearing a blue suit and gray shirt and had a gun at 10 Exchange Place.
    C. At 10:00 A.M., Clayton Pelt, owner of The Diamond Dome Jewelry Store, which is located at 10 Exchange Place, was robbed of a $50,000 diamond ring at gunpoint. The suspect is a white male with black hair wearing a blue suit and gray shirt.
    D. In a robbery that occurred at gunpoint, a white male with black hair robbed The Diamond Dome Jewelry Store, which is located at 10 Exchange Place. Clayton Pelt, the owner who was robbed of a $50,000 diamond ring, said he was wearing a blue suit and a gray shirt at 10:00 A.M.

11.____

12. Dispatcher Sanders receives the following information from the computer: Place of Occurrence: Bushwick Housing Projects, rear of Building 12B
Time of Occurrence: 6:00 P.M.
Crime: Mugging
Victim: Hispanic female
Suspect: Unknown

Dispatcher sanders is about to relay the information to the patrol car.
Which one of the following expresses the above information MOST clearly and accurately?

12.____

A. In the rear of Building 12B, a Hispanic female was mugged. An unknown suspect was in the Bushwick Housing Projects at 6:00 P.M.

B. At 6:00 P.M., a Hispanic female was mugged by an unknown suspect in the rear of Building 12B, in the Bushwick Housing Projects.

C. At 6:00 P.M., a female is in the rear of Building 12B in the Bushwick Housing Projects. An unknown suspect mugged a Hispanic female.

D. A suspect's identity is unknown in the rear of Building 12B in the Bushwick Housing Project at 6:00 P.M. A Hispanic female was mugged.

Questions 13-15.

DIRECTIONS: Questions 13 through 15 are to be answered SOLELY on the basis of the following passage.

Dispatcher Clark, who is performing a 7:30 A.M. to 3:30 P.M. tour of duty, receives a call from Mrs. Gold. Mrs. Gold states there are four people selling drugs in front of Joe's Cleaners, located at the intersection of Main Street and Broadway. After checking the location in the computer, Dispatcher Clark asks the caller to give a description of each person. She gives the following descriptions: one white male wearing a yellow shirt, green pants, and red sneakers; one Hispanic male wearing a red and white shirt, black pants, and white sneakers; one black female wearing a green and red striped dress and red sandals; and one black male wearing a green shirt, yellow pants, and green sneakers. She also states that the Hispanic male, who is standing near a blue van, has the drugs inside a small black shoulder bag. She further states that she saw the black female hide a gun inside a brown paper bag and place it under a black car parked in front of Joe's Cleaners. The drug selling goes on everyday at various times. During the week, it occurs from 7 A.M. to 1 P.M. and from 5 P.M. to 12 A.M., but on weekends it occurs from 3 P.M. until 7 A.M.

13. Which person was wearing red sneakers?   13.____

    A. Black male   B. Hispanic male
    C. Black female   D. White male

14. Mrs. Gold stated the drugs were located   14.____

    A. under the blue van
    B. inside the black shoulder bag
    C. under the black car
    D. inside the brown paper bag

15. At what time does Mrs. Gold state the drugs are sold on weekends?   15.____

    A. 7:30 A.M. - 3:30 P.M.   B. 7:00 A.M. - 1:00 P.M.
    C. 5:00 P.M. - 12:00 A.M.   D. 3:00 P.M. - 7:00 A.M.

16. Police Communications Technician Bentley receives a call of an auto being stripped. He   16.____
    obtains the following information from the caller:
    Place of Occurrence: Corner of West End Avenue and W. 72nd Street
    Time of Occurrence: 10:30 P.M.
    Witness: Mr. Simpson
    Suspects: Two white males
    Crime: Auto stripping
    Action Taken: Suspects fled before police arrived

27

Communications Technician Bentley is about to enter the incident into the computer and send the information to the dispatcher.

Which one of the following expresses the above information MOST clearly and accurately?

    A.   At 10:30 P.M., Mr. Simpson witnessed two white males stripping an auto parked at the corner of West End Avenue and W. 72nd Street. The suspects fled before the police arrived.

    B.   An auto was parked at the corner of West End Avenue and W. 72nd Street. Two white males who were stripping at 10:30 P.M. were witnessed by Mr. Simpson. Before the police arrived, the suspects fled.

    C.   Mr. Simpson saw two white males at the corner of West End Avenue and W. 72nd Street. Fleeing the scene before the police arrived, the witness saw the suspects strip an auto.

    D.   Before the police arrived at 10:30 P.M. on the corner of West End Avenue and W. 72nd Street, Mr. Simpson witnessed two white males. The suspects, who stripped an auto, fled the scene.

17.   911 Operator Washington receives a call of a robbery and obtains the following information regarding the incident: 17.____

Place of Occurrence:	First National Bank, 45 West 96th Street
Time of Occurrence:	2:55 P.M.
Amount Taken:	$10,000
Description of Suspect:	Male, black, wearing a leather jacket, blue jeans, and white shirt
Weapon:	Gun

911 Operator Washington is about to enter the call into the computer.

Which one of the following expresses the above information MOST clearly and accurately?

    A.   At 2:55 P.M., the First National Bank, located at 45 West 96th Street, was robbed at gunpoint of $10,000. The suspect is a black male and is wearing a leather jacket, blue jeans, and a white shirt.

    B.   Ten thousand dollars was robbed from the First National Bank at 2:55 P.M. A black male was wearing a leather jacket, blue jeans, and a white shirt at 45 West 96th Street. He also had a gun.

    C.   At 2:55 P.M., a male was wearing a leather jacket, blue jeans, and a white shirt. The First National Bank located at 45 West 96th Street was robbed by a black male. Ten thousand dollars was taken at gunpoint.

    D.   Robbing the First National Bank, a male wore a leather jacket, blue jeans, and a white shirt at gunpoint. A black male was at 45 W. 96th Street. At 2:55 P.M., $10,000 was taken.

Questions 18-20.

DIRECTIONS: Questions 18 through 20 are to be answered SOLELY on the basis of the following passage.

Police Communications Technician Gordon receives a call from a male stating there is a bomb set to explode in the gym of Public School 85 in two hours. Realizing the urgency of the call, the Communications Technician calls the radio dispatcher, who assigns Patrol Car 43A to the scene. Communications Technician Gordon then notifies her supervisor, Miss Smith, who first reviews the tape of the call, then calls the Operations Unit which is notified of all serious incidents, and she reports the facts. The Operations Unit notifies the Mayor's Information Agency and Borough Headquarters of the emergency situation.

18. Who did Communications Technician Gordon notify FIRST?　　　　　　　　18._____

   A. Supervisor Smith　　　　　B. Operations Unit
   C. Patrol Car 43A　　　　　　D. Radio dispatcher

19. The Operations Unit was notified　　　　　　　　　　　　　　　　　　19._____

   A. to inform school personnel of the bomb
   B. so they can arrive at the scene before the bomb is scheduled to go off
   C. to evacuate the school
   D. due to the seriousness of the incident

20. Who did Miss Smith notify?　　　　　　　　　　　　　　　　　　　　20._____

   A. Patrol Car 43A
   B. Operations Unit
   C. Mayor's Information Agency
   D. Borough Headquarters

———————

KEY (CORRECT ANSWERS)

1.	D	11.	C
2.	C	12.	B
3.	A	13.	D
4.	A	14.	B
5.	C	15.	D
6.	A	16.	A
7.	D	17.	A
8.	B	18.	D
9.	C	19.	D
10.	C	20.	B

———————

TEST 2

DIRECTIONS: Each question or incomplete statement is followed by several suggested answers or completions. Select the one that BEST answers the question or completes the statement. *PRINT THE LETTER OF THE CORRECT ANSWER IN THE SPACE AT THE RIGHT.*

1. A Police Communications Technician receives a call reporting a large gathering. She obtained the following information:

   Place of Occurrence: Cooper Square Park
   Time of Occurrence: 1:15 A.M.
   Occurrence: Youths drinking and playing loud music
   Complainant: Mrs. Tucker, 20 Cooper Square
   Action Taken: Police scattered the crowd

   Communications Technician Carter is about to relay the information to the dispatcher. Which one of the following expresses the above information MOST clearly and accurately?

   A. The police responded to Cooper Square Park because Mrs. Tucker, who called 911, lives at 20 Cooper Square. The group of youths was scattered due to drinking and playing loud music at 1:15 A.M.
   B. Mrs. Tucker, who lives at 20 Cooper Square, called 911 to make a complaint of a group of youths who were drinking and playing loud music in Cooper Square Park at 1:15 A.M. The police responded and scattered the crowd.
   C. Loud music and drinking in Cooper Square Park by a group of youths caused the police to respond and scatter the crowd. Mrs. Tucker called 911 and complained. At 1:15 A.M., she lives at 20 Cooper Square.
   D. Playing loud music and drinking, Mrs. Tucker called the police. The police scattered a group of youths in Cooper Square Park at 1:15 A.M. Mrs. Tucker lives at 20 Cooper Square.

1.____

2. Dispatcher Weston received a call from the owner of a gas station and obtained the following information:

   Place of Occurrence: Blin's Gas Station, 1800 White Plains Road
   Time of Occurrence: 10:30 A.M.
   Occurrence: Left station without paying
   Witness: David Perilli
   Description of Auto: A white Firebird, license plate GEB275
   Suspect: Male, white, wearing blue jeans and a black T-shirt

   Dispatcher Weston is about to enter the information into the computer. Which one of the following expresses the above information MOST clearly and accurately?

   A. At 10:30 A.M., David Perilli witnessed a white male wearing blue jeans and a black T-shirt leave Blin's Gas Station, located at 1800 White Plains Road, without paying. The suspect was driving a white Firebird with license plate GEB275.
   B. Wearing blue jeans and a black T-shirt, David Perilli witnessed a white male leave Blin's Gas Station without paying. He was driving a white Firebird with license plate GEB275. This occurred at 1800 White Plains Road at 10:30 A.M.
   C. David Perilli witnessed a male wearing blue jeans and a black T-shirt driving a white Firebird. At 10:30 A.M., a white male left Blin's Gas Station, located at 1800 White Plains Road, without paying. His license plate was GEB275.

2.____

D. At 10:30 A.M., David Perilli witnessed a white male leaving Blin's Gas Station without paying. The driver of a white Firebird, license plate GEB275, was wearing blue jeans and a black T-shirt at 1800 White Plains Road.

Questions 3-4.

DIRECTIONS: Questions 3 and 4 are to be answered SOLELY on the basis of the following information.

Police Communications Technicians are required to assist callers who need non-emergency assistance. The callers are referred to non-emergency agencies. Listed below are some non-emergency situations and the agencies to which they should be referred.

Agency
Local Precinct
Environmental Protection Agency
Sanitation Department
S.P.C.A.
Transit Authority

Unoccupied suspicious car
Open fire hydrant
Abandoned car
Injured, stray or sick animal
Transit Authority travel information

3. Communications Technician Carter received a call from Mr. Cane, who stated that a car without license plates had been parked in front of his house for five days. Mr. Crane should be referred to the

A. A.S.P.C.A.
B. Transit Authority
C. Sanitation Department
D. Environmental Protection Agency

3.____

4. Mrs. Dunbar calls to report that a dog has been hit by a car and is lying at the curb in front of her house. Mrs. Dunbar should be referred to the

A. Sanitation Department
B. Local Precinct
C. Environmental Protection Agency
D. A.S.P.C.A.

4.____

5. Operator Bryant received a call of a robbery and obtained the following information:

Place of Occurrence: Deluxe Deli, 303 E. 30th Street
Time of Occurrence: 5:00 P.M.
Crime: Robbery of $300
Victim: Bonnie Smith, cashier of Deluxe Deli
Description of Suspect: White, female, blonde hair, wearing black slacks and a red shirt
Weapon: Knife

Operator Bryant is about to enter this information into the computer.
Which one of the following expresses the above information MOST clearly and accurately?

5.____

A. Bonnie Smith, the cashier of the Deluxe Deli reported at 5:00 P.M. that she was robbed of $300 at knifepoint at 303 East 30th Street. A white female with blonde hair was wearing black slacks and a red shirt.

B. At 5:00 P.M., a blonde-haired female robbed the 303 East 30th Street store. At the Deluxe Deli, cashier Bonnie Smith was robbed of $300 by a white female at knife-point. She was wearing black slacks and a red shirt.

C. In a robbery that occurred at knifepoint, a blonde-haired white female robbed $300 from the Deluxe Deli. Bonnie Smith, cashier of the 303 East 30th Street store, said she was wearing black slacks and a red shirt at 5:00 P.M.

D. At 5:00 P.M., Bonnie Smith, cashier of the Deluxe Deli, located at 303 East 30th Street, was robbed of $300 at knifepoint. The suspect is a white female with blonde hair wearing black slacks and a red shirt.

6. 911 Operator Landers receives a call reporting a burglary that happened in the past. He obtained the following information from the caller:

Place of Occurrence:	196 Simpson Street
Date of Occurrence:	June 12
Time of Occurrence:	Between 8:30 A.M. and 7:45 P.M.
Victim:	Mr. Arnold Frank
Items Stolen:	$300 cash, stereo, assorted jewelry, and a VCR

911 Operator Landers is about to enter the incident into the computer.
Which one of the following expresses the above information MOST clearly and accurately?

6.____

A. Mr. Arnold Frank stated that on June 12, between 8:30 A.M. and 7:45 P.M., someone broke into his home at 196 Simpson Street and took $300 in cash, a stereo, assorted jewelry, and a VCR.

B. Mr. Arnold Frank stated between 8:30 A.M. and 7:45 P.M., he lives at 196 Simpson Street. A stereo, VCR, $300 in cash, and assorted jewelry were taken on June 12.

C. Between 8:30 A.M. and 7:45 P.M. on June 12, Mr. Arnold Frank reported someone broke into his home. At 196 Simpson Street, a VCR, $300 in cash, a stereo, and assorted jewelry were taken.

D. A stereo, VCR, $300 in cash, and assorted jewelry were taken between 8:30 M. and 7:45 P.M. On June 12, Mr. Arnold Frank reported he lives at 196 Simpson Street.

Questions 7-9.

DIRECTIONS: Questions 7 through 9 are to be answered SOLELY on the basis of the following passage.

Communications Operator Harris receives a call from Mrs. Stein who reports that a car accident occurred in front of her home. She states that one of the cars belongs to her neighbor, Mrs. Brown, and the other car belongs to Mrs. Stein's son, Joseph Stein. Communications Operator Harris enters Mrs. Stein's address into the computer and receives information that no such address exists. She asks Mrs. Stein to repeat her address. Mrs. Stein repeats her address and states that gasoline is leaking from the cars and that smoke is coming from their engines. She further states that people are trapped in the cars and then hangs up.

Communications Operator Harris notifies her supervisor, Jones, that she received a call but was unable to verify the address and that the caller hung up. Mrs. Jones listens to the tape of the call and finds that the caller stated 450 Park Place not 415 Park Place. She advises Communications Operator Harris to enter the correct address, then notify Emergency Service Unit to respond to the individuals trapped in the cars, the Fire Department for the smoke condition, and Emergency Medical Service for any possible injuries.

7. Who did Communications Operator Harris notify concerning the problem with the caller's address?   7._____

    A. Mrs. Brown   B. Joseph Stein
    C. Joseph Brown   D. Mrs. Jones

8. Which agency was Communications Operator Harris advised to notify concerning individuals trapped in the cars?   8._____

    A. Emergency Medical Service
    B. Fire Department
    C. Emergency Service Unit
    D. NYC Police Department

9. Which agency did Supervisor Jones advise Communications Operator Harris to notify for the smoke condition?   9._____

    A. NYC Police Department
    B. Emergency Medical Service
    C. Fire Department
    D. Emergency Service Unit

Question 10.

DIRECTIONS: Question 10 is to be answered SOLELY on the basis of the following information.

When a Police Communications Technician receives a call concerning a bank robbery, a Communications Technician should do the following in the order given:

    I.   Get address and name of the bank from the caller.
    II.   Enter the address into the computer.
    III.   Use the *Hotline* button to alert the dispatcher of the serious incident going into the computer.
    IV.   Get back to the caller and get the description of the suspect and other pertinent information.
    V.   Enter additional information into the computer and send it to the dispatcher.
    VI.   Upgrade the seriousness of the incident so it appears first on dispatcher's screen.
    VII.   Notify the Supervising Police Communications Technician of the bank robbery.

10. Police Communications Technician Brent receives a call from Mr. Ross stating that while   10.____
he was on line at the Trust Bank, at West 34th Street and 9th Avenue, he witnessed a
bank robbery. Communications Technician Brent enters the address into the computer,
then presses the *Hotline* button and alerts the dispatcher that there was a bank robbery
at the Trust Bank on West 34th Street and 9th Avenue. Mr. Ross continues to state that
the robber is a white male in his 30's wearing a light blue shirt and blue jeans.
After obtaining other pertinent information, the NEXT step Communications Technician
Brent should take is to

    A. enter additional information into the computer and send it to the dispatcher
    B. upgrade the seriousness of the incident so it appears first on the dispatcher's
       screen
    C. notify his supervisor of the bank robbery
    D. use the *Hotline* button to alert the dispatcher of a serious incident going into the
       computer

11. Dispatcher Wilson receives a call regarding drugs being sold in the lobby of an apart-   11.____
ment building. He obtains the following information:

Place of Occurrence: 305 Willis Avenue
Time of Occurrence: 2:00 P.M.
Witnesses: Roy Rodriguez and Harry Armstrong
Suspect: Melvin Talbot, left the scene before the police arrived
Crime: Drug sale

Dispatcher Wilson is about to enter this incident into the computer.
Which one of the following expresses the above information MOST clearly and accurately?

    A. Roy Rodriguez and Harry Armstrong reported that they witnessed Melvin Talbot
       selling drugs in the lobby of 305 Willis Avenue at 2:00 P.M. The suspect left the
       scene before the police arrived.
    B. In the lobby, Roy Rodriguez reported at 2:00 P.M. he saw Melvin Talbot selling
       drugs with Harry Armstrong. He left the lobby of 305 Willis Avenue before the
       police arrived.
    C. Roy Rodriguez and Harry Armstrong witnessed drugs being sold at 305 Willis Ave-
       nue. Before the police arrived at 2:00 P.M., Melvin Talbot left the lobby.
    D. Before the police arrived, witnesses stated that Melvin Talbot was selling drugs. At
       305 Willis Avenue, in the lobby, Roy Rodriguez and Harry Armstrong said he left
       the scene at 2:00 P.M.

12. Operator Rogers receives a call of a car being stolen. He obtains the following informa-   12.____
tion:

Place of Occurrence: Parking lot at 1723 East 20th Street
Time of Occurrence: 2:30 A.M.
Vehicle Involved: 1988 Toyota Corolla
Suspects: Male, Hispanic, wearing a red T-shirt
Crime: Auto theft
Witness: Janet Alonzo

Operator Rogers is entering the information into the computer.
Which one of the following expresses the above information MOST clearly and accurately?

34

A. At 2:30 A.M., wearing a red T-shirt, Janet Alonzo witnessed a 1988 Toyota Corolla being stolen by a male Hispanic in the parking lot at 1723 East 20th Street.
B. A male Hispanic, wearing a red T-shirt, was in the parking lot at 1723 East 20th Street." At 2:30 A.M., Janet Alonzo witnessed a 1988 Toyota Corolla being stolen.
C. At 2:30 A.M., Janet Alonzo witnessed a 1988 Toyota Corolla in the parking lot at 1723 East 20th Street being stolen by a male Hispanic who is wearing a red T-shirt.
D. Janet Alonzo witnessed a 1988 Toyota Corolla in the parking lot being stolen. At 2:30 A.M., a male Hispanic was wearing a red T-shirt at 1723 East 20th Street.

Question 13.

DIRECTIONS: Question 13 is to be answered SOLELY on the basis of the following information.

There are times when Police Communications Technicians have to reassign officers in a patrol car from a less serious incident which does not require immediate police response to an incident of a more serious nature which does require immediate police response. Police Communications Technicians must choose among the assigned patrol cars and determine which one is assigned to the least serious incident, then reassign that one to the situation which requires immediate police response.

Communications Technician Reese is working the 13th Division which covers the 79th Precinct. There are only four patrol cars working in the 79th Precinct. They are assigned as follows:

79A is assigned to a car accident with injuries involving an intoxicated driver.

79B is assigned to a group of teenagers playing loud music in a park.

79C is assigned to a group of teenagers trying to steal liquor in a liquor store, who are possibly armed with guns.

79D is assigned to a suspicious man in a bank, with possible intentions to rob the bank.

13. If Communications Technician Reese receives a call of an incident that requires immediate police response, which patrol car should be reassigned?   13._____

A. 79A   B. 79B   C. 79C   D. 79D

Questions 14-16.

DIRECTIONS: Questions 14 through 16 are to be answered SOLELY on the basis of the following information.

On May 12, at 3:35 P.M., Police Communications Technician Connor receives a call from a child caller requesting an ambulance for her mother, whom she cannot wake. The child did not know her address, but gave Communications Technician Connor her apartment number and telephone number. Communications Technician Connor's supervisor, Ms. Bendel, is advised of the situation and consult's Cole's Directory, a listing published by the Bell Telephone Company, to obtain an address when only the telephone number is known. The telephone number is unlisted. Ms. Bendel asks Communications Technician Taylor to call Telco Security to obtain an address from their telephone number listing. Communications Technician Taylor speaks to Ms. Morris of Telco Security and obtains the address. Communications Technician Connor, who is still talking with the child, is given the address by Communications Technician Taylor. She enters the information into the computer system and transfers the caller to the Emergency Medical Service.

14. What information did Communications Technician Connor obtain from the child caller?   14._____

    A. Telephone number and apartment number
    B. Name and address
    C. Address and telephone number
    D. Apartment number and address

15. Communications Technician Taylor obtained the address from   15._____

    A. Communications Technician Connor
    B. Ms. Morris
    C. Supervisor Bendel
    D. the child caller

16. The caller's address was obtained by calling   16._____

    A. Cole's Directory
    B. Telco Security
    C. Emergency Medical Service
    D. The Telephone Company

Question 17.

DIRECTIONS: Question 17 is to be answered SOLELY on the basis of the following information.

The following incidents appear on the Police Communications Technician's computer screen which were called in by three different callers at the same time:

    I. At 3040 Hill Avenue between Worth and Centre Streets, there are two people fighting in the third floor hallway. One of them has a shiny metal object.
    II. In a building located on Hill Avenue between Worth and Centre Streets, a man and a woman are having an argument on the third floor. The woman has a knife in her hand.
    III. In front of Apartment 3C on the third floor, a husband and wife are yelling at each other. The wife is pointing a metal letter opener at her husband. The building is located on the corner of Hill Avenue and Worth Street.

17. A Police Communications Technician may be required to combine into one incident many calls that appear on the computer screen if they seem to be reporting the same incident. Which of the above should a Police Communications Technician combine into one incident?   17._____

    A. I and II
    C. II and III
            B. I and III
            D. I, II, and III

Questions 18-19.

DIRECTIONS: Questions 18 and 19 are to be answered SOLELY on the basis of the following
information.

Police Communications Technicians must be able to identify and assign codes to the
crimes described in the calls they receive. All crimes are coded by number and by priority. The
priority code number indicates the seriousness of the crime. The lower the priority number, the
more serious the crime.

Listed below is a chart of several crimes and their definitions. The corresponding crime
code and priority code number are given.

CRIME	DEFINITION	CRIME CODE	PRIORITY CODE
Criminal Mischief:	Occurs when a person intentionally damages another person's property	29	6
Harrassment:	Occurs when a person intentionally annoys another person by striking, shoving, or kicking them without causing injury	27	8
Aggravated Harrassment:	Occurs when a person intentionally annoys another person by using any form of communication	28	9
Theft of Service:	Occurs when a person intentionally avoids payment for services given	25	7

18.   Communications Technician Rogers received a call from Mrs. Freeman, who stated that   18._____
her next door neighbor, whom she had an argument with, has thrown a rock through her
apartment window.
Which one of the following is the CORRECT crime code?

     A. 29   B. 28   C. 27   D. 25

19.   Communications Technician Tucker received a call from a man who stated that he is a   19._____
waiter at the Frontier Diner. He states that one of his customers was refusing to pay for
his meal.
Which one of the following is the CORRECT priority code number for this crime?

     A. 6   B. 7   C. 8   D. 9

Dispatcher Matthews received a call of a bomb threat. He obtained the following infor-   19._____
mation;
Address of Occurrence: 202 Church Avenue
Location: 2nd floor men's room
Time of Call: 12:00 P.M.
Time of Occurrence: 2:00 P.M.
Terrorist Organization: People *Against Government*

Caller: Anonymous male member of *People* Against Government
Action Taken: Supervisor Jones notified of the bomb threat
Dispatcher Matthews is about to enter the information into the computer.
Which one of the following expresses the above information MOST clearly and accurately?

- A. An anonymous male called Dispatcher Matthews and told him that a bomb is set to go off at 202 Church Avenue in the 2nd floor men's room at 2:00 P.M. Dispatcher Matthews notified Supervisor Jones that the caller is from *People Against Government* at 12:00 P.M.
- B. Dispatcher Matthews received a call in the 2nd floor men's room of a bomb threat from an anonymous male member of the *People Against Government* terrorist organization. He notified Supervisor Jones at 12:00 P.M. that a bomb is set to go off at 2:00 P.M. at 202 Church Avenue.
- C. Dispatcher Matthews received a call at 202 Church Avenue from the *People Against Government*, a terrorist organization. An anonymous male stated that a bomb is set to go off at 2:00 P.M. in the 2nd floor men's room. At 12:00 P.M., Dispatcher Matthews notified Supervisor Jones of the call.
- D. At 12:00 P.M., Dispatcher Matthews received a call from an anonymous male caller who states that he is from a terrorist organization known as *People Against Government*. He states that a bomb has been placed in the 2nd floor men's room of 202 Church Avenue and is set to go off at 2:00 P.M. Dispatcher Matthews notified Supervisor Jones of the bomb threat.

KEY (CORRECT ANSWERS)

1.	B		11.	A
2.	A		12.	C
3.	C		13.	B
4.	D		14.	A
5.	D		15.	B
6.	A		16.	B
7.	D		17.	D
8.	C		18.	A
9.	C		19.	B
10.	A		20.	D

EXAMINATION SECTION
TEST 1

DIRECTIONS: Each question or incomplete statement is followed by several suggested answers or completions. Select the one that BEST answers the question or completes the statement. *PRINT THE LETTER OF THE CORRECT ANSWER IN THE SPACE AT THE RIGHT.*

1. You are operating the switchboard and you receive an outside call for an extension line which is busy.
The one of the following which you should do FIRST is to

   A. ask the caller to try again later
   B. ask the caller to wait and inform him every thirty seconds about the status of the extension line
   C. tell the caller the line is busy and ask him if he wishes to wait
   D. tell the caller the line is busy and that you will connect him as soon as possible

1.____

2. A person comes to your work area. He makes comments which make no sense, gives foolish opinions, and tells you that he has enemies who are after him. He appears to be mentally ill.
Of the following, the FIRST action to take is to

   A. humor him by agreeing and sympathizing with him
   B. try to reason with him and point out that his fears or opinions are unfounded
   C. have him arrested immediately
   D. tell him to leave at once

2.____

3. You are speaking with someone on the telephone who asks you a question which you cannot answer. You estimate that you can probably obtain the requested information in about five minutes.
Of the following, the MOST appropriate course of action would be to tell the caller that

   A. the information will take a short while to obtain, and then ask her for her name and number so that you can call her back when you have the information
   B. the information is available now, but she should call back later
   C. you do not know the answer and refer her to another division you think might be of service
   D. she is being placed on *hold* and that you will be with her in about five minutes

3.____

4. A person with a very heavy foreign accent comes to your work area and starts talking to you. He is very excited and is speaking too rapidly for you to understand what he is saying.
Of the following, the FIRST action for you to take is to

   A. refer the person to your supervisor
   B. continue your work and ignore the person in the hope that he will be discouraged and leave the building
   C. ask or motion to the person to speak more slowly and have him repeat what he is trying to communicate
   D. assume that the person is making a complaint, tell him that his problem will be taken care of, and then go back to your work

4.____

5. Assume that you are responsible for handling supplies. You notice that you are running low on a particular type of manila file folder exceptionally fast. You believe that someone in the precinct is taking the folders for other than official use.
In this situation, the one of the following that you should do FIRST is to

    A. put up a notice stating that supplies have been disappearing and ask for the staff's cooperation in eliminating the problem
    B. speak to your supervisor about the matter and let him decide on a course of action
    C. watch the supply cabinet to determine who is taking the folders
    D. ignore the situation and put in a requisition for additional folders

5.____

6. One afternoon, several of the officers ask you to perform different tasks. Each task requires a half day of work. Each officer tells you that his assignment must be finished by 4 P.M. the next day.
Of the following, the BEST way to handle this situation is to

    A. do the assignments as quickly as you can, in the order in which the officers handed them to you
    B. do some work on each assignment in the order of the ranks of the assigning officers and hand in as much as you are able to finish
    C. speak to your immediate supervisor in order to determine the priority of assignments
    D. accept all four assignments but explain to the last officer that you may not be able to finish his job

6.____

7. Every morning, several officers congregate around your work station during their breaks. You find their conversations very distracting.
The one of the following which you should do FIRST is to

    A. ask them to cooperate with you by taking their breaks somewhere else
    B. concentrate as best you can because their breaks do not last very long
    C. reschedule your break to coincide with theirs
    D. tell your supervisor that the officers are very uncooperative

7.____

8. One evening when you are very busy, you answer the phone and find that you are speaking with one of the neighborhood cranks, an elderly man who constantly complains that his neighbors are noisy.
In this situation, the MOST appropriate action for you to take is to

    A. hang up and go on with your work
    B. note the complaint and process it in the usual way
    C. tell the man that his complaint will be investigated and then forget about it
    D. tell the man that you are very busy and ask him to call back later

8.____

9. One morning you answer a telephone call for Lieutenant Jones, who is busy on another line. You inform the caller that Lieutenant Jones is on another line and this party says he will hold. After two minutes, Lieutenant Jones is still speaking on the first call.
Of the following, the FIRST thing for you to do is to

    A. ask the second caller whether it is an emergency
    B. signal Lieutenant Jones to let him know there is another call waiting for him
    C. request that the second caller try again later
    D. inform the second caller that Lieutenant Jones' line is still busy

9.____

10. The files in your office have been overcrowded and difficult to work with since you started working there. One day your supervisor is transferred and another aide in your office decides to discard three drawers of the oldest materials.
For him to take this action is

    A. *desirable;* it will facilitate handling the more active materials
    B. *undesirable;* no file should be removed from its point of origin
    C. *desirable;* there is no need to burden a new supervisor with unnecessary information
    D. *undesirable;* no file should be discarded without first noting what material has been discarded

10._____

11. You have been criticized by the lieutenant-in-charge because of spelling errors in some of your typing. You have only copied the reports as written, and you realize that the errors occurred in work given to you by Sergeant X.
Of the following, the BEST way for you to handle this situation is to

    A. tell the lieutenant that the spelling errors are Sergeant X's, not yours, because they occur only when you type his reports
    B. tell the lieutenant that you only type the reports as given to you, without implicating anyone
    C. inform Sergeant X that you have been unjustly criticized because of his spelling errors and politely request that he be more careful in the future
    D. use a dictionary whenever you have doubt regarding spelling

11._____

12. You have recently found several items misfiled. You believe that this occurred because a new administrative aide in your section has been making mistakes.
The BEST course of action for you to take is to

    A. refile the material and say nothing about it
    B. send your supervisor an anonymous note of complaint about the filing errors
    C. show the errors to the new administrative aide and tell him why they are errors in filing
    D. tell your supervisor that the new administrative aide makes a lot of errors in filing

12._____

13. One of your duties is to record information on a standard printed form regarding missing cars. One call you receive concerns a custom-built auto which has apparently been stolen. There seems to be no place on the form for many of the details which the owner gives you.
Of the following, the BEST way for you to obtain an adequate description of this car would be to

    A. complete the form as best you can and attach another sheet containing the additional information the owner gives you
    B. complete the form as best you can and request that the owner submit a photograph of the missing car
    C. scrap the form since it is inadequate in this case and make out a report based on the information the owner gives you
    D. complete the form as best you can and ignore extraneous information that the form does not call for

13._____

14. One weekend, you develop a painful infection in one hand. You know that your typing speed will be much slower than normal, and the likelihood of your making mistakes will be increased.
Of the following, the BEST course of action for you to take in this situation is to

    A. report to work as scheduled and do your typing assignments as best you can without complaining
    B. report to work as scheduled and ask your co-workers to divide your typing assignments until your hand heals
    C. report to work as scheduled and ask your supervisor for non-typing assignments until your hand heals
    D. call in sick and remain on medical leave until your hand is completely healed so that you can perform your normal duties

14.____

15. When filling out a departmental form during an interview concerning a citizen complaint, an administrative aide should know the purpose of each question that he asks the citizen.
For such information to be supplied by the department is

    A. *advisable*, because the aide may lose interest in the job if he is not fully informed about the questions he has to ask
    B. *inadvisable*, because the aide may reveal the true purpose of the questions to the citizens
    C. *advisable*, because the aide might otherwise record superficial or inadequate answers if he does not fully understand the questions
    D. *inadvisable*, because the information obtained through the form may be of little importance to the aide

15.____

16. Which one of the following is NOT a generally accepted rule of telephone etiquette for an administrative aide?

    A. Answer the telephone as soon as possible after the first ring
    B. Speak in a louder than normal tone of voice, on the assumption that the caller is hard-of-hearing
    C. Have a pencil and paper ready at all times with which to make notes and take messages
    D. Use the tone of your voice to give the caller the impression of cooperativeness and willingness to be of service

16.____

17. The one of the following which is the BEST reason for placing the date and time of receipt of incoming mail is that this procedure

    A. aids the filing of correspondence in alphabetical order
    B. fixes responsibility for promptness in answering correspondence
    C. indicates that the mail has been checked for the presence of a return address
    D. makes it easier to distribute the mail in sequence

17.____

18. Which one of the following is the FIRST step that you should take when filing a document by subject? 18.____

    A. Arrange related documents by date with the latest date in front
    B. Check whether the document has been released for filing
    C. Cross-reference the document if necessary
    D. Determine the category under which the document will be filed

19. The one of the following which is NOT generally employed to keep track of frequently used material requiring future attention is a 19.____

    A. card tickler file
    B. dated follow-up folder
    C. periodic transferral of records
    D. signal folder

20. Assume that a newly appointed administrative aide arrives 15 minutes late for the start of his tour of duty. One of his co-workers tells him not to worry because he has signed him in on time. The co-worker assures him that he would be willing to cover for him anytime he is late and hopes the aide will do the same for him. The aide agrees to do so. This arrangement is 20.____

    A. *desirable;* it prevents both men from getting a record for tardiness
    B. *undesirable;* signing in for each other is dishonest
    C. *desirable;* cooperation among co-workers is an important factor in morale
    D. *undesirable;* they will get caught if one is held up in a lengthy delay

21. An administrative aide takes great pains to help a citizen who approaches him with a problem. The citizen thanks the aide curtly and without enthusiasm. Under these circumstances, it would be MOST courteous for the aide to 21.____

    A. tell the citizen he was glad to be of service
    B. ask the citizen to put the compliment into writing and send it to his supervisor
    C. tell the citizen just what pains he took to render this service so that the citizen will be fully aware of his efforts
    D. make no reply and ignore the citizen's remarks

22. Assume that your supervisor spends a week training you, a newly appointed administrative aide, to sort fingerprints for filing purposes. After doing this type of filing for several days, you get an idea which you believe would improve upon the method in use. Of the following, the BEST action for you to take in this situation is to 22.____

    A. wait to see whether your idea still looks good after you have had more experience
    B. try your idea out before bringing it up with your supervisor
    C. discuss your idea with your supervisor
    D. forget about this idea since the fingerprint sorting system was devised by experts

23. Which one of the following is NOT a useful filing practice? 23.____

    A. Filing active records in the most accessible parts of the file cabinet
    B. Filling a file drawer to capacity in order to save space
    C. Gluing small documents to standard-size paper before filing
    D. Using different colored labels for various filing categories

43

24. A citizen comes in to make a complaint to an administrative aide.
The one of the following actions which would be the MOST serious example of discourtesy would be for the aide to

    A.   refuse to look up from his desk even though he knows someone is waiting to speak to him
    B.   not use the citizen's name when addressing him once his identity has been ascertained
    C.   interrupt the citizen's story to ask questions
    D.   listen to the complaint and refer the citizen to a special office

24.____

25. Suppose that one of your neighbors walks into the precinct where you are an administrative aide and asks you to make 100 copies of a letter on the office duplicating machine for his personal use.
Of the following, what action should you take FIRST in this situation?

    A.   Pretend that you do not know the person and order him to leave the building
    B.   Call a police officer and report the person for attempting to make illegal use of police equipment
    C.   Tell the person that you will copy the letter but only when you are off duty
    D.   Explain to the person that you cannot use police equipment for non-police work

25.____

———

KEY (CORRECT ANSWERS)

1.	C	11.	D
2.	A	12.	C
3.	A	13.	A
4.	C	14.	C
5.	B	15.	C
6.	C	16.	B
7.	A	17.	B
8.	B	18.	B
9.	D	19.	C
10.	D	20.	B

21.	A
22.	C
23.	B
24.	A
25.	D

———

TEST 2

DIRECTIONS: Each question or incomplete statement is followed by several suggested answers or completions. Select the one that BEST answers the question or completes the statement. *PRINT THE LETTER OF THE CORRECT ANSWER IN THE SPACE AT THE RIGHT.*

Questions 1-6.

DIRECTIONS: Questions 1 through 6 are to be answered on the basis of the information supplied in the chart below.

LAW ENFORCEMENT OFFICERS KILLED
(By Type of Activity)

2006-2015

LAW ENFORCEMENT OFFICERS KILLED
(By Type of Activity)

```
                                                    2006-2010 [      ]
                                                    2011-2015 [IIIIII]

RESPONDING TO
DISTURBANCE CALLS                                            48
                                                             50

BURGLARIES IN PROGRESS                              28
OR PURSUING BURGLARY SUSPECT                        25

ROBBERIES IN PROGRESS                                        48
OR PURSUING ROBBERY SUSPECT                                      74

ATTEMPTING OTHER ARRESTS                                        56
                                                                    112

CIVIL DISORDERS                      2
                                     8

HANDLING, TRANSPORTING,              12
CUSTODY OF PRISONERS                 17

INVESTIGATING SUSPICIOUS             28
PERSONS AND CIRCUMSTANCES            29

AMBUSH                               13
                                     29

UNPROVOKED                           5
MENTALLY DERANGED                    20

TRAFFIC STOPS                        10
                                     19
```

45

1. According to the above chart, the percent of the total number of law enforcement officers killed from 2006-2015 in activities related to burglaries and robberies is MOST NEARLY _____ percent.

   A. 8.4   B. 19.3   C. 27.6   D. 36.2

2. According to the above chart, the two of the following categories which increased from 2006-10 to 2011-15 by the same percent are

   A. ambush and traffic stops
   B. attempting other arrests and ambush
   C. civil disorders and unprovoked mentally deranged
   D. response to disturbance calls and investigating suspicious persons and circumstances

3. According to the above chart, the percentage increase in law enforcement officers killed from the 2006-10 period to the 2011-15 period is MOST NEARLY _____ percent.

   A. 34   B. 53   C. 65   D. 100

4. According to the above chart, in which one of the following activities did the number of law enforcement officers killed increase by 100 percent?

   A. Ambush
   B. Attempting other arrests
   C. Robberies in progress or pursuing robbery suspect
   D. Traffic stops

5. According to the above chart, the two of the following activities during which the total number of law enforcement officers killed from 2006 to 2015 was the same are

   A. burglaries in progress or pursuing burglary suspect and investigating suspicious persons and circumstances
   B. handling, transporting, custody of prisoners and traffic stops
   C. investigating suspicious persons and circumstances and ambush
   D. responding to disturbance calls and robberies in progress or pursuing robbery suspect

6. According to the categories in the above chart, the one of the following statements which can be made about law enforcement officers killed from 2006 to 2010 is that

   A. the number of law enforcement officers killed during civil disorders equals one-sixth of the number killed responding to disturbance calls
   B. the number of law enforcement officers killed during robberies in progress or pursuing robbery suspect equals 25 percent of the number killed while handling or transporting prisoners
   C. the number of law enforcement officers killed during traffic stops equals one-half the number killed for unprovoked reasons or by the mentally deranged
   D. twice as many law enforcement officers were killed attempting other arrests as were killed during burglaries in progress or pursuing burglary suspect

Questions 7-10.

DIRECTIONS: Assume that all arrests fall into two mutually exclusive categories, felonies and misdemeanors. Last week 620 arrests were made in Precinct A, of which 403 were for felonies. Questions 7 through 10 are to be answered on the basis of this information.

7. The percent of all arrests made in Precinct A last week which were for felonies was _____ percent.

    A. 55   B. 60   C. 65   D. 70

7._____

8. If 3/5 of all persons arrested for felonies and 1/4 of all persons arrested for misdemeanors were carrying weapons, then the number of arrests involving persons carrying weapons in Precinct A last week was MOST NEARLY

    A. 135   B. 295   C. 415   D. 525

8._____

9. If five times as many men as women were arrested for felonies, and half as many women as men were arrested for misdemeanors, then the number of women arrested in Precinct A last week was APPROXIMATELY

    A. 90   B. 120   C. 175   D. 210

9._____

10. If the ratio of arrests made on weekends (Friday through Sunday) to arrests made on weekdays (Monday through Thursday) is 2:1, then the number of arrests made in . Precinct A last weekend was

    A. 308   B. 340   C. 372   D. 413

10._____

11. The police precincts covering the county receive calls at the average rate of two per minute during the 8 A.M. to 4 P.M. tour, but this rate increases by 50 percent during the 4 P.M. to 12 A.M. tour. However, the initial rate decreases by 50 percent during the 12 A.M. to 8 A.M. tour.
The number of calls received by the precincts covering the county on this basis in one 24-hour day is

    A. 960   B. 1440   C. 2880   D. 3360

11._____

12. If an administrative aide is expected to handle 15 calls per hour and Precinct C averages 840 calls during the 4 P.M. to 12 A.M. tour, then the number of aides needed in Precinct C to handle calls during this tour is

    A. 4   B. 5   C. 6   D. 7

12._____

13. If in a group of ten administrative aides, four type 40 words per minute, one types 45, two type 50, two type 60, and one types 65, then the average speed in the group is _____ words per minute.

    A. 49   B. 50   C. 51   D. 52

13._____

14. An administrative aide works from midnight to 8 A.M. on a certain day and then is off for 64 hours.
He is due back at work at

    A. 8 A.M.   B. 12 noon
    C. 4 P.M.   D. 12 midnight

14._____

15. If a certain aide takes one hour to type 2 accident reports or 6 missing person reports, then the length of time he will require to finish 7 accident reports and 15 missing persons reports is _____ hours _____ minutes.   15._____

    A. 6; 0   B. 6; 30   C. 8; 0   D. 8; 40

16. If one administrative aide can alphabetize 320 reports per hour and another can do 280 per hour, then the number of reports that both could alphabetize during an 8-hour tour is   16._____

    A. 4800   B. 5200   C. 5400   D. 5700

17. If 1000 candidates applied for administrative aide, and out of those applying 7/8 appear for the written test, and out of those who take the written test 66 2/3 percent pass it, and out of those who pass the written test 85 percent pass the medical exam, then the number of candidates still eligible to become administrative aides will be about   17._____

    A. 245   B. 495   C. 585   D. 745

18. If the number of murders in the city in 1980 was 415, and the number of murders has increased by 8 percent each year since that year, then in 1983 we would expect the number of murders to be about   18._____

    A. 484   B. 523   C. 548   D. 565

19. If a person reported missing on April 15 was found murdered on July 4, how many days was he missing? (Include April 15 but NOT July 4 in the total.)   19._____

    A. 76   B. 80   C. 82   D. 84

20. Suppose that a pile of 96 file cards measures one inch in height and that it takes you 1/2 hour to file these cards away.
If you are given three piles of cards which measure 2 1/2 inches high, 1 3/4 inches high, and 3 3/8 inches high, respectively, the time it would take to file the cards is MOST NEARLY _____ hours and _____ minutes.   20._____

    A. 2; 30   B. 3; 50   C. 6; 45   D. 8; 15

Questions 21-30.

DIRECTIONS: Questions 21 through 30 test how good you are at catching mistakes in typing or printing. In each question, the name and addresses in Column I should be an exact copy of the name and address in Column I.
Mark your answer
    A. if there is no mistake in either name or address
    B. if there is a mistake in both name and address
    C. if there is a mistake only in the name
    D. if there is a mistake only in the address

COLUMN I   COLUMN II

21. Milos Yanocek   Milos Yanocek   21._____
    33-60 14 Street   33-60 14 Street
    Long Island City, NY 11011   Long Island City, NY 11001

22. Alphonse Sabattelo
24 Minnetta Lane
New York, NY 10006

Alphonse Sabbattelo
24 Minetta Lane
New York, NY 10006

22._____

23. Helen Stearn
5 Metropolitan Oval
Bronx, NY 10462

Helene Stearn
5 Metropolitan Oval
Bronx, NY 10462

23._____

24. Jacob Weisman
231 Francis Lewis Boulevard
Forest Hills, NY 11325

Jacob Weisman
231 Francis Lewis Boulevard
Forest Hill, NY 11325

24._____

25. Riccardo Fuente
135 West 83 Street
New York, NY 10024

Riccardo Fuentes
134 West 88 Street
New York, NY 10024

25._____

26. Dennis Lauber
52 Avenue D
Brooklyn, NY 11216

Dennis Lauder
52 Avenue D
Brooklyn, NY 11216

26._____

27. Paul Cutter
195 Galloway Avenue
Staten Island, NY 10356

Paul Cutter
175 Galloway Avenue
Staten Island, NY 10365

27._____

28. Sean Donnelly
45-58 41 Avenue
Woodside, NY 11168

Sean Donnelly
45-58 41 Avenue
Woodside, NY 11168

28._____

29. Clyde Willot
1483 Rockaway Avenue
Brooklyn, NY 11238

Clyde Willat
1483 Rockway Avenue
Brooklyn, NY 11238

29._____

30. Michael Stanakis
419 Sheriden Avenue
Staten Island, NY 10363

Michael Stanakis
419 Sheraden Avenue
Staten Island, NY 10363

30._____

Questions 31-40.

DIRECTIONS: Questions 31 through 40 are to be answered only on the basis of the following information.

Column I consists of serial numbers of dollar bills. Column II shows different ways of arranging the corresponding serial numbers.

The serial numbers of dollar bills in Column I begin and end with a capital letter and have an eight-digit number in between. The serial numbers in Column I are to be arranged according to the following rules:

First: In alphabetical order according to the first letter
Second: When two or more serial numbers have the same first letter, in alphabetical order according to the last letter

Third: When two or more serial numbers have the same first and last letters, in numerical order, beginning with the lowest number.

The serial numbers in Column I are numbered (1) through (5) in the order in which they are listed. In Column II, the numbers (1) through (5) are arranged in four different ways to show different arrangements of the corresponding serial numbers. Choose the answer in Column II in which the serial numbers are arranged according to the above rules.

SAMPLE QUESTION:

	COLUMN I		COLUMN II
(1)	E75044127B	(A)	4, 1, 3, 2, 5
(2)	B96399104A	(B)	4, 1, 2, 3,5
(3)	B93939086A	(C)	4,3, 2, 5,1
(4)	B47064465H	(D)	3, 2, 5, 4,1
(5)	B99040922A		

In the sample question, the four serial numbers starting with B should be put before the serial numbers starting with E. The serial numbers starting with B and ending with A should be put before the serial number starting with B and ending with H. The three serial numbers starting with B and ending with A should be listed in numerical order, beginning with the lowest number. The correct way to arrange the serial numbers, therefore, is

(3) B93939086A
(2) B96399104A
(5) B99040922A
(4) B47064465H
(1) E75044127B

Since the order of arrangement is 3, 2, 5, 4, 1, the answer to the sample question is (D).

	COLUMN I		COLUMN II	
31.	(1) P44343314Y	A.	2, 3, 1, 4, 5	31.____
	(2) P44141341S	B.	1, 5, 3, 2, 4	
	(3) P44141431L	C.	4, 2, 3, 5, 1	
	(4) P41143413W	D.	5, 3, 2, 4, 1	
	(5) P44313433H			
32.	(1) D89077275M	A.	3, 2, 5, 3, 1	32.____
	(2) D98073724N	B.	1, 4, 3, 2, 5	
	(3) D90877274N	C.	4, 1, 5, 2, 3	
	(4) D98877275M	D.	1, 3, 2, 5, 3	
	(5) D98873725N			
33.	(1) H32548137E	A.	2, 4, 5, 1, 3	33.____
	(2) H35243178A	B.	1, 5, 2, 3, 4	
	(3) H35284378F	C.	1, 5, 2, 4, 3,	
	(4) H35288337A	D.	2, 1, 5, 3, 4	
	(5) H32883173B			

34. (1) K24165039H
    (2) F24106599A
    (3) L21406639G
    (4) C24156093A
    (5) K24165593D

   A. 4, 2, 5, 3, 1
   B. 2, 3, 4, 1, 5
   C. 4, 2, 5, 1, 3
   D. 1, 3, 4, 5, 2

34._____

35. (1) H79110642E
    (2) H79101928E
    (3) A79111567F
    (4) H79111796E
    (5) A79111618F

   A. 2, 1, 3, 5, 4
   B. 2, 1, 4, 5, 3
   C. 3, 5, 2, 1, 4
   D. 4, 3, 5, 1, 2

35._____

36. (1) P16388385W
    (2) R16388335V
    (3) P16383835W
    (4) R18386865V
    (5) P18686865W

   A. 3, 4, 5, 2, 1
   B. 2, 3, 4, 5, 1
   C. 2, 4, 3, 1, 5
   D. 3, 1, 5, 2, 4

36._____

37. (1) B42271749G
    (2) B42271779G
    (3) E43217779G
    (4) B42874119C
    (5) E42817749G

   A. 4, 1, 5, 2, 3
   B. 4, 1, 2, 5, 3
   C. 1, 2, 4, 5, 3
   D. 5, 3, 1, 2, 4

37._____

38. (1) M57906455S
    (2) N87077758S
    (3) N87707757B
    (4) M57877759B
    (5) M57906555S

   A. 4, 1, 5, 3, 2
   B. 3, 4, 1, 5, 2
   C. 4, 1, 5, 2, 3
   D. 1, 5, 3, 2, 4

38._____

39. (1) C69336894Y
    (2) C69336684V
    (3) C69366887W
    (4) C69366994Y
    (5) C69336865V

   A. 2, 5, 3, 1, 4
   B. 3, 2, 5, 1, 4
   C. 3, 1, 4, 5, 2
   D. 2, 5, 1, 3, 4

39._____

40. (1) A56247181D
    (2) A56272128P
    (3) H56247128D
    (4) H56272288P
    (5) A56247188D

   A. 1, 5, 3, 2, 4
   B. 3, 1, 5, 2, 4
   C. 3, 2, 1, 5, 4
   D. 1, 5, 2, 3, 4

40._____

Questions 41-48.

DIRECTIONS: Questions 41 through 48 are to be answered only on the basis of the following passage.

Auto theft is prevalent and costly. In 2015, 486,000 autos valued at over $500 million were stolen. About 28 percent of the inhabitants of Federal prisons are there as a result of conviction of interstate auto theft under the Dyer Act. In California alone, auto thefts cost the criminal justice system approximately $60 million yearly.

The great majority of auto theft is for temporary use rather than resale, as evidenced by the fact that 88 percent of autos stolen in 2015 were recovered. In Los Angeles, 64 percent of stolen autos that were recovered were found within two days and about 80 percent within a week. Chicago reports that 71 percent of the recovered autos were found within four miles of the point of theft. The FBI estimates that 8 percent of stolen cars are taken for the purpose of stripping them for parts, 12 percent for resale, and 5 percent for use in another crime. Auto thefts are primarily juvenile acts. Although only 21 percent of all arrests for nontraffic offenses in 2015 were of individuals under 18 years of age, 63 percent of auto theft arrests were of persons under 18. Auto theft represents the start of many criminal careers; in an FBI sample of juvenile auto theft offenders, 41 percent had no prior arrest record.

41. In the passage above, the discussion of the reasons for auto theft does NOT include the percent of   41._____

    A.   autos stolen by prior offenders
    B.   recovered stolen autos found close to the point of theft
    C.   stolen autos recovered within a week
    D.   stolen autos which were recovered

42. Assuming the figures in the above passage remain constant, you may logically estimate the cost of auto thefts to the California criminal justice system over a five-year period beginning in 2015 to have been about _____ million.   42._____

    A. $200   B. $300   C. $440   D. $500

43. According to the above passage, the percent of stolen autos in Los Angeles which were not recovered within a week was _____ percent.   43._____

    A. 12   B. 20   C. 29   D. 36

44. According to the above passage, MOST auto thefts are committed by   44._____

    A.   former inmates of Federal prisons
    B.   juveniles
    C.   persons with a prior arrest record
    D.   residents of large cities

45. According to the above passage, MOST autos are stolen for   45._____

    A.   resale   B.   stripping of parts
    C.   temporary use   D.   use in another crime

46. According to the above passage, the percent of persons arrested for auto theft who were under 18   46._____

    A.   equals nearly the same percent of stolen autos which were recovered
    B.   equals nearly two-thirds of the total number of persons arrested for nontraffic offenses
    C.   is the same as the percent of persons arrested for nontraffic offenses who were under 18
    D.   is three times the percent of persons arrested for nontraffic offenses who were under 18

47. An APPROPRIATE title for the above passage is

47.____

    A. How Criminal Careers Begin
    B. Recovery of Stolen Cars
    C. Some Statistics on Auto Theft
    D. The Costs of Auto Theft

48. Based on the above passage, the number of cars taken for use in another crime in 1995 was

48.____

    A. 24,300   B. 38,880   C. 48,600   D. 58,320

Questions 49-55.

DIRECTIONS: Questions 49 through 55 are to be answered only on the basis of the following passage.

    Burglar alarms are designed to detect intrusion automatically. Robbery alarms enable a victim of a robbery or an attack to signal for help. Such devices can be located in elevators, hallways, homes and apartments, businesses and factories, and subways, as well as on the street in high-crime areas. Alarms could deter some potential criminals from attacking targets so protected. If alarms were prevalent and not visible, then they might serve to suppress crime generally. In addition, of course, the alarms can summon the police when they are needed.

    All alarms must perform three functions: sensing or initiation of the signal, transmission of the signal, and annunciation of the alarm. A burglar alarm needs a sensor to detect human presence or activity in an unoccupied enclosed area like a building or a room. A robbery victim would initiate the alarm by closing a foot or wall switch, or by triggering a portable transmitter which would send the alarm signal to a remote receiver. The signal can sound locally as a loud noise to frighten away a criminal, or it can be sent silently by wire to a central agency. A centralized annunciator requires either private lines from each alarmed point, or the transmission of some information on the location of the signal.

49. A conclusion which follows LOGICALLY from the above passage is that

49.____

    A. burglar alarms employ sensor devices; robbery alarms make use of initiation devices
    B. robbery alarms signal intrusion without the help of the victim; burglar alarms require the victim to trigger a switch
    C. robbery alarms sound locally; burglar alarms are transmitted to a central agency
    D. the mechanisms for a burglar alarm and a robbery alarm are alike

50. According to the above passage, alarms can be located

50.____

    A. in a wide variety of settings
    B. only in enclosed areas
    C. at low cost in high-crime areas
    D. only in places where potential criminals will be deterred

51. According to the above passage, which of the following is ESSENTIAL if a signal is to be received in a central office? 51.____

    A. A foot or wall switch
    B. A noise producing mechanism
    C. A portable reception device
    D. Information regarding the location of the source

52. According to the above passage, an alarm system can function WITHOUT a 52.____

    A. centralized annunciating device
    B. device to stop the alarm
    C. sensing or initiating device
    D. transmission device

53. According to the above passage, the purpose of robbery alarms is to 53.____

    A. find out automatically whether a robbery has taken place
    B. lower the crime rate in high-crime areas
    C. make a loud noise to frighten away the criminal
    D. provide a victim with the means to signal for help

54. According to the above passage, alarms might aid in lessening crime if they were 54.____

    A. answered promptly by police
    B. completely automatic
    C. easily accessible to victims
    D. hidden and widespread

55. Of the following, the BEST title for the above passage is 55.____

    A. Detection of Crime by Alarms
    B. Lowering the Crime Rate
    C. Suppression of Crime
    D. The Prevention of Robbery

KEY (CORRECT ANSWERS)

1. C	11. C	21. D	31. D	41. A	51. D
2. C	12. D	22. B	32. B	42. B	52. A
3. B	13. A	23. C	33. A	43. B	53. D
4. B	14. D	24. A	34. C	44. B	54. D
5. B	15. A	25. B	35. C	45. C	55. A
6. D	16. A	26. C	36. D	46. D	
7. C	17. B	27. D	37. B	47. C	
8. B	18. B	28. A	38. A	48. A	
9. C	19. B	29. B	39. A	49. A	
10. D	20. B	30. D	40. D	50. A	

READING COMPREHENSION
UNDERSTANDING AND INTERPRETING WRITTEN MATERIAL

EXAMINATION SECTION
TEST 1

DIRECTIONS: Each question or incomplete statement is followed by several suggested answers or completions. Select the one that BEST answers the question or completes the statement. *PRINT THE LETTER OF THE CORRECT ANSWER IN THE SPACE AT THE RIGHT.*

Questions 1-12.

DIRECTIONS: Questions 1 through 12 are to be answered SOLELY on the basis of the following passage.

Police Officers Bret Clemens and Sam Harte are dispatched to 83-67 Richardson Boulevard, Apt. 23F, at 8:53 P.M., on November 18 in response to a burglary reported by a Mr. Kegler. They arrive at the apartment at 8:58 P.M., ring the doorbell, and are greeted by Mr. and Mrs. Kegler. Mr. Kegler tells the Officers that he left for his foreman's job at the telephone company at 7:00 A.M., and that his wife left for her secretary's job 10 minutes later. After work, Mr. Kegler picked up his wife, and they returned to their apartment at 8:40 P.M., having eaten dinner out. When Mrs. Kegler entered the bedroom, she noticed her jewelry box on the floor. She told her husband, who then called the police. While the Keglers waited for the police to arrive, they discovered that all of Mrs. Kegler's jewelry and Mr. Kegler's coin collection, as well as approximately $175.00 in cash, were missing.

While Officer Harte begins to fill out a crime report, Officer Clemens goes to other apartments on the same floor to interview neighbors who might have additional information about the burglary.

Mrs. Johnston, age 35, a housewife, who lives in Apt. 23C located directly opposite the elevator, tells Officer Clemens that she heard voices in the hallway outside her apartment door at 4:30 P.M. She thought that the voices were those of a neighbor's children who sometimes play in the hallway. She opened her door to chase them away but, instead, saw two strange males standing by the elevator. They wore green work clothes. She noticed that the taller man was white, about 28 years old, 5'11", 165 lbs., with brown hair and was carrying a square leather case. The other man was Hispanic, about 21 years old, 5'7", 150 lbs., with black hair and a scar on the left side of his face.

Officer Clemens then contacts other residents at Apartments 23D, 23E, and 23G. All of them tell the Officer that they did not see or hear anything unusual. Officer Clemens then returns to the Keglers' apartment to tell his partner what he learned. In the meantime, Officer Harte had been told by Mr. Kegler that his coin collection was in a square brown leather carrying case.

Officer Harte was also told that Mr. Kegler is 42 years old. His telephone number at work is 827-6138, and his work address is 273 Eastern Avenue. Mrs. Kegler's telephone number at work is 746-3279, and her work address is 131 South Moore Street. The Keglers' home telephone number is 653-3946. Mrs. Johnston's telephone number at home is 653-2714.

Officers Harte and Clemens finish their investigation and complete the crime report.

1. Which one of the following is the APPROXIMATE time that the two strange men were seen in the hallway?

   A. 7:00 A.M.   B. 4:30 P.M.   C. 8:40 P.M.   D. 8:53 P.M.

2. Which one of the following apartments is directly opposite the elevator?

   A. 23B   B. 23C   C. 23F   D. 23G

3. Which one of the following is Mrs. Kegler's work address?

   A. 273 Eastern Avenue   B. 653 Eastern Avenue
   C. 131 South Moore Street   D. 746 South Moore Street

4. Which one of the following was NOT stolen during the burglary of the Keglers' apartment?

   A. $175.00
   B. Mrs. Kegler's jewelry
   C. Mr. Kegler's coin collection
   D. Credit cards

5. When did the Keglers return to their apartment?
   _____ P.M.

   A. 8:40   B. 8:45   C. 8:53   D. 8:58

6. What is Mrs. Kegler's occupation?

   A. Housewife   B. Supervisor
   C. Secretary   D. Unknown

7. What is Mr. Kegler's telephone number at work?

   A. 653-2714   B. 746-3279   C. 653-3946   D. 827-6138

8. What is the approximate age of the TALLER of the two strangers seen standing near the elevator?

   A. 21   B. 28   C. 42   D. 57

9. Which one of the following is the MOST accurate description of the male stranger who was seen near the elevator carrying the leather case?

   A. 5'7" and 165 lbs., Hispanic, brown hair
   B. 5'11" and 150 lbs., White, black hair
   C. 5'7" and 150 lbs., Hispanic, black hair
   D. 5'11" and 165 lbs., White, brown hair

10. Which one of the following identifying marks is part of the description of the shorter male stranger seen standing near the elevator?

    A. Scar   B. Tattoo   C. Birthmark   D. Mole

10._____

11. Mr. Kegler's employer is the _____ company.

    A. electric   B. jewelry   C. gas   D. telephone

11._____

12. At what time did Mrs. Kegler leave for work?
    _____ A.M.

    A. 7:00   B. 7:10   C. 7:30   D. 8:40

12._____

Questions 13-14.

DIRECTIONS: Questions 13 and 14 are to be answered SOLELY on the basis of the following passage. Officer Pei is told to notify the station house when he spots dangerous conditions.

13. Which one of the following should the Officer report?
    A

    A. car with a stuck horn parked on a side street
    B. broken traffic light at a busy intersection
    C. car, double-parked in front of a newspaper stand, with its flashers on
    D. truck unloading vegetable crates into a supermarket

13._____

14. Which one of the following should the Officer report?
    A

    A. scaffold on the sixteenth floor of an office building containing two men washing the windows
    B. crane moving girders to the ground floor of a building under construction
    C. man working on a chimney of a three-story house
    D. section of roof about to fall on the street from a two-story house

14._____

Questions 15-25.

DIRECTIONS: Questions 15 through 25 are to be answered SOLELY on the basis of the following passage.

    Police Officers Tom Riggins and John Landry were patrolling in their police car in the 65th Precinct at 10:15 A.M. on December 3, 1993. They came upon the scene of a traffic accident at Avenue C and 30th Street, which had occurred five minutes earlier. Officer Landry called the Police Radio Dispatcher at 10:20 A.M. and reported that he and his partner in Police Car #65B were handling a traffic accident involving a van and an auto at that location. Officer Landry further reported to the Dispatcher that there were no personal injuries to the van driver or to the driver of the auto or her two children. However, the two vehicles were damaged.

The Officers checked each driver's license, vehicle registration certificate, and vehicle insurance identification card. The van driver was John Hudson, age 36, residing at 1102 South Elliot Boulevard, Cranford, N.J. He was driving a white 1987 GMC van, N.Y. license plate #9723GH, owned by his employer, Zenith Trucking Corp. of 257 West 63rd Street, N.Y., N.Y. Mr. Hudson's N.J. driver's license identification number is H138569, and the expiration date is December 31, 1993.

The driver of the auto was Mrs. Anne Cloris, age 38, residing at 49 Christopher Avenue, Queens, N.Y. She had two children with her, Charles Cloris, Jr., age 10, and Anita Cloris, age 8. Mrs. Cloris' auto was a red 1989 Chevrolet 4-door station wagon, N.Y. license plate #319GAZ. Mrs. Cloris' N.Y. driver's license identification number is C12192-16619, and the expiration date is May 31, 1995.

The Officers examined both vehicles for damage from the accident and found that the van had a dented rear panel on its left side and that the auto had a dented right front fender.

The Officers completed a vehicle accident report at 10:45 A.M. The report number was V4359.

15. Which one of the following is the CORRECT description of the vehicles involved in the traffic accident?
    One _____ and one _____.

    A. van; 4-door station wagon
    B. 4-door station wagon; trailer truck
    C. 2-door station wagon; van
    D. van; 4-door sedan

15._____

16. Which one of the following is the CORRECT license plate number and description of Mrs. Cloris' vehicle?
    N.Y. plate #

    A. 319GAZ, white 1987 Chevrolet van
    B. 319GZA, red 1989 GMC station wagon
    C. 319GAZ, red 1989 Chevrolet station wagon
    D. 318GAZ, white 1989 Chevrolet van

16._____

17. At what time did the traffic accident occur?
    _____ A.M.

    A. Before 10:00   B. 10:10
    C. 10:15   D. 10:20

17._____

18. How many personal injuries resulted from the traffic accident?

    A. 0   B. 1   C. 2   D. 3

18._____

19. Which one of the following is the age of Charles Cloris, Jr.?

    A. 8   B. 10   C. 12   D. Unknown

19._____

20. Which one of the following is Mrs. Cloris' N.Y. driver's license identification number?

    A. H315869   B. H138569
    C. C12291-16619   D. C12192-16619

20._____

21. Which one of the following is the license plate number of Mr. Hudson's vehicle? 21._____

   A. 9724GH   B. 9723GH   C. 9724HG   D. 9723HG

22. Which one of the following is the expiration date of Mr. Hudson's driver's license? 22._____

   A. December 30, 1993   B. December 31, 1993
   C. May 30, 1994   D. May 31, 1994

23. Which one of the following is the address of Mr. Hudson's residence? 23._____

   A. 1201 South Elliot Boulevard, Cranford, N.J.
   B. 1102 South Elliot Avenue, Cranford, N.Y.
   C. 1102 South Elliot Boulevard, Cranford, N.J.
   D. 1102 North Elliot Boulevard, Cranford, N.Y.

24. Which one of the following is the address of Mr. Hudson's employer? 24._____

   A. 257 West 63rd Street, N.Y., N.Y.
   B. 49 Christopher Avenue, Queens, N.Y.
   C. 263 West 57th Street, N.Y., N.Y.
   D. 94 Christopher Street, Queens, N.Y.

25. Which one of the following is the CORRECT description of the damage to Mr. Hudson's vehicle from the accident? 25._____
A dented

   A. right front fender   B. left rear panel
   C. left rear fender   D. right front panel

KEY (CORRECT ANSWERS)

1.	B		11.	D
2.	B		12.	B
3.	C		13.	B
4.	D		14.	D
5.	A		15.	A
6.	C		16.	C
7.	D		17.	B
8.	B		18.	A
9.	D		19.	B
10.	A		20.	D

21.	B
22.	B
23.	C
24.	A
25.	B

TEST 2

DIRECTIONS: Each question or incomplete statement is followed by several suggested answers or completions. Select the one that BEST answers the question or completes the statement. *PRINT THE LETTER OF THE CORRECT ANSWER IN THE SPACE AT THE RIGHT.*

Questions 1-4.

DIRECTIONS: Questions 1 through 4 are to be answered SOLELY on the basis of the following passage.

At 11:55 A.M., Police Officer Benson was on foot patrol on 44th Street between 6th Avenue and Broadway. This post is known to be a high crime area with a large number of narcotics, robbery, and prostitution arrests. Police Officer Benson approached a young woman he had previously arrested for prostitution. As he was about to question her, he heard a scream coming from the direction of a women's boutique on the opposite side of the street. A young Black male was running up 44th Street towards Broadway, followed by a woman yelling, *Stop that man!* Police Officer Benson ran after the woman but by the time he caught up with her, she had fallen after tripping on the badly cracked sidewalk. The woman was visibly shaken and appeared to have broken her arm. Police Officer Benson decided that because the young Black male had disappeared from sight, he should stay with the injured woman and call for an ambulance. While awaiting the arrival of the ambulance, the injured woman, Ms. Peever, told Police Officer Benson that she was the owner of the boutique and that the young Black male had taken approximately $475 from the cash register while she went to check the price of an item. She also mentioned that the boutique was presently unattended because her two sales people had not come to work that morning.

Police Officer Benson called for back-up assistance at 12:35 P.M. and asked the dispatcher to send a police officer directly to the boutique located at 338 West 44th Street. Police Officers Maloney and Hernandez arrived at the boutique at 1:05 P.M. and saw that the store had been ransacked. Racks of clothing had been thrown down, and the floor was littered with garments. The two Police Officers then conducted a search of the premises. When Police Officer Benson arrived at the premises at 1:20 P.M., the Police Officers told him that it would be impossible to determine what items had been taken since they had no listing of the store's merchandise.

A young woman then entered the store and identified herself as Ms. Peake, the part-time assistant whose shift started at 1:30 P.M. On seeing the condition of the store, she asked the Police Officers what had happened. They asked her where the merchandise list for the store was kept, and she informed them that the stock clerks, Ms. Feldman and Mr. Austin, kept that information. Ms. Peake said that she would call Ms. Feldman in order to get a current listing of the store's merchandise.

Ms. Peake advised the Police Officers that several items were missing from the display case, including three fur jackets, seven leather handbags, and four silk blouses, amounting to at least $985 in value.

1. At which one of the following addresses is the boutique located?   1.____

    A. 388 East 44th Street   B. 44th Street and Broadway

    C. 338 West 44th Street   D. 44th Street and 6th Ave.

2. At what time did Police Officer Benson meet Police Officers Maloney and Hernandez at   2.____
the boutique?
_____ P.M.

    A. 12:35   B. 12:55   C. 1:05   D. 1:20

3. Which one of the following people owns the boutique?   3.____

    A. Ms. Peever   B. Mr. Austin

    C. Ms. Feldman   D. Ms. Peake

4. What is Ms. Peake's starting time at the boutique?   4.____
_____ P.M.

    A. 12:35   B. 1:05   C. 1:20   D. 1:30

Questions 5-8.

DIRECTIONS: Questions 5 through 8 are to be answered SOLELY on the basis of the following passage.

Housing Police Officer Jones, Shield #691, assigned to foot patrol at Borinquen Plaza Housing Project and working a 4 P.M. to 12 P.M. tour on September 17, 1994, received a call from the police radio dispatcher at 6:10 P.M. to respond to 60 Moore Street, Apt. 7E, on a case involving an elderly woman in need of medical assistance.

Police Officer Jones stated to the dispatcher that he would respond but on two previous occasions he was called to that same location and the woman refused medical treatment.

Police Officer Jones arrived at 60 Moore Street at 6:15 P.M., took the elevator to the 7th floor, and walked over to Apartment 7E. The Police Officer found the apartment door open, and inside he found the woman, her daughter, and two paramedics. The paramedics had arrived five minutes before the Police Officer. Paramedics Smith #2634 and Hanson #1640 stated to Police Officer Jones that the woman identified as Maria Rivera, age 64, date of birth 5/29/30, who was lying on a dirty mattress in her bedroom, was in shock and in need of medical treatment, but she was refusing medical aid.

Police Officer Jones could not convince Mrs. Rivera to go to the hospital to receive medical treatment. Mrs. Aida Soto, age 32, daughter of Mrs. Rivera, who resides at 869 Flushing Avenue, Apt. 11F, was also present, but she too was unable to convince her mother to go to the hospital.

Police Officer Jones called the police radio dispatcher at 6:25 P.M. and requested the Housing Supervisor to respond to the location. The Housing Supervisor, Sergeant Cuevas, Shield #664, arrived at 6:40 P.M., and Police Officer Jones informed him of the situation. Sergeant Cuevas spoke to Mrs. Rivera and her daughter in Spanish but could not get either to agree that Mrs. Rivera needed urgent medical treatment. Sergeant Cuevas directed paramedics Smith and Hanson to take Mrs. Rivera to the hospital.

Mrs. Rivera was removed from the apartment at 7:00 P.M. and was put in ambulance #1669 and taken to Greenwood Hospital. The ambulance arrived at the hospital at 7:10 P.M., and Mrs. Rivera received the medical treatment she so urgently needed.

Police Officer Jones and Sergeant Cuevas resumed normal patrol at 7:12 P.M. Police Officer Jones prepared Field Report #8964 before the end of his tour.

5. Which one of the following is the CORRECT time that Police Officer Jones arrived at 60 Moore Street?
   _____ P.M.

   A. 6:10   B. 6:15   C. 6:45   D. 7:15

   5.____

6. Which one of the following is the CORRECT apartment to which Police Officer Jones responded?

   A. 11F   B. 7F   C. 11E   D. 7E

   6.____

7. Which one of the following is the CORRECT birthdate of Mrs. Rivera?

   A. 5/19/30   B. 5/29/30   C. 7/30/33   D. 8/5/30

   7.____

8. Which one of the following is the CORRECT name of the sick woman's daughter?

   A. Aida Soto   B. Aida Rivera
   C. Maria Rivera   D. Anna Soto

   8.____

Questions 9-10.

DIRECTIONS: Questions 9 and 10 are to be answered SOLELY on the basis of the following passage.

Police officers are sometimes required to respond to the scene of a traffic accident involving two vehicles. In situations in which one of the drivers involved in the accident has driven away from the scene before the officer arrives, the responding police officer must use the following procedures in the order given:
   I. Ask the driver of the remaining vehicle if he noticed the license plate number of the vehicle which fled.
      A. If license plate number is known, call Vehicle Inquiry Section to determine name and address of owner.
      B. Write down the name and the address of owner of vehicle which fled.
      C. Give name and address of owner of vehicle which fled to driver remaining at scene of accident.
   II. Obtain from driver remaining at scene all details of the accident including description of vehicle which fled.
   III. Call Stolen Vehicle Desk.
   IV. Prepare Complaint Form in duplicate upon return to precinct.
   V. Give original of Complaint Form to Sergeant.
   VI. Place copy of Complaint Form in Vehicle Complaint Folder.

9. Police Officer Mica arrives at the scene of a traffic accident involving two cars. One of the drivers fled the scene five minutes before Mica arrived, but the driver of the remaining vehicle, Henry Bates, was able to see the fleeing vehicle's license plate number and reports it to Mica.
   Which one of the following actions should Police Officer Mica take NEXT?

   9.____

   A. Prepare Complaint Form in duplicate.
   B. Call Stolen Vehicle Desk.
   C. Give original of Complaint Form to Sergeant.
   D. Call Vehicle Inquiry Section.

10. Five minutes later, Police Officer Mica has already completed all the appropriate actions through obtaining from Bates all details of the accident and a description of the fleeing vehicle.
    Which one of the following actions should Police Officer Mica take NEXT?

    10.____

    A. Call Stolen Vehicle Desk.
    B. Call Vehicle Inquiry Section.
    C. Prepare Complaint Form in duplicate.
    D. Place copy of Complaint Form in Vehicle Complaint Folder.

Questions 11-12.

DIRECTIONS: Questions 11 and 12 are to be answered SOLELY on the basis of the following passage.

At 11 o'clock on Sunday morning, Police Officer Dempsey arrives on the scene of a vehicle accident that had happened approximately 30 minutes earlier involving a school bus carrying 20 children traveling north on Sumpter Ave.; a cement truck traveling south on Sumpter Ave.; a car traveling east on Swan Blvd.; and a motorcycle traveling west on Swan Blvd. The Officer asks the people standing around at the scene if any of them had seen the accident take place. The following is what each of those who claimed to have seen the accident take place said.

Mr. W: I was walking my dog at 10:30 when I saw a cement truck that was traveling on Sumpter Ave. swerve to miss a stalled car in the intersection of Sumpter and Swan, and hit a school bus traveling in the opposite direction. The bus in turn spun around and hit a car traveling on Swan, which in turn hit a motorcycle, also on Swan.

Miss X: At 10:30, I was on my way to work when I heard a loud screeching of brakes. I immediately looked around and saw a cement truck swerve, miss a stalled car in the intersection of Sumpter and Swan, hit a school bus, which in turn hit a car on Swan. The car then collided with a motorcycle on Swan. I saw a man jump out of the cement truck and run down Sumpter.

Mrs. Y: I was returning home after having bought a bottle of whiskey from the corner liquor store when I saw a cement truck going down Sumpter hit its brakes, swerve around a car that had stalled, and collide with a school bus. The school bus then hit into a car and motorcycle that were on Swan.

65

<u>Mr. Z</u>: I was in my house which is located on the corner of Sumpter and Swan when I heard a crash. I looked out and saw a cement truck and school bus that apparently had collided at the intersection of Sumpter and Swan. I then saw that a car and motorcycle on Swan had been involved in the accident as well. There was a stalled car in the intersection.

11. The Officer should report that there are errors in the statements made by one or more of the above four people concerning which one of the following elements?   11.____

    A.   The number of vehicles involved in the accident
    B.   The location of the accident
    C.   Their activities prior to the accident
    D.   The time the accident took place

12. Whose account of the accident includes a possibly important element NOT mentioned by the others?   12.____

    A. Mr. W   B. Miss X   C. Mrs. Y   D. Mr. Z

Questions 13-20.

DIRECTIONS: Questions 13 through 20 are based on the following excerpt from a recorded annual report of the police department. This material should be read first and then referred to in answering these questions, which are to be answered SOLELY on the basis of the material herein contained.

LEGAL BUREAU

One of the more important functions of this bureau is to analyze and furnish the department with pertinent information concerning Federal and State statutes and Local Laws which affect the department, law enforcement or crime prevention. In addition, all measures introduced in the State Legislature and the City Council which may affect this department are carefully reviewed by members of the Legal Bureau and, where necessary, opinions and recommendations thereon are prepared.

Another important function of this office is the prosecution of cases in the Magistrate's Courts. This is accomplished by assignment of attorneys who are members of the Legal Bureau to appear in those cases which are deemed to raise issues of importance to the department or questions of law which require technical presentation to facilitate proper determination; and also in those cases where request is made for such appearances by a magistrate, some other official of the city, or a member of the force. Attorneys are regularly assigned to prosecute all cases in the Women's Court.

Proposed legislation was prepared and sponsored for introduction in the State Legislature and, at this writing, one of these proposals has already been enacted into law and five others are presently on the Governor's desk awaiting executive action. The new law prohibits the sale or possession of a hypodermic syringe or needle by an unauthorized person. The bureau's proposals awaiting executive action pertain to an amendment to the Code of Criminal Procedure prohibiting desk officers from taking bail in gambling cases or in cases mentioned in Section 552, Code of Criminal Procedure; including confidence men and swindlers as jostlers in the Penal Law; prohibiting the sale of switchblade knives of any size to children under 16, and bills extending the licensing period of gunsmiths.

The Legal Bureau has regularly cooperated with the Corporation Counsel and the District Attorneys in respect to matters affecting this department, and has continued to advise and represent the Police Athletic League, the Police Sports Association, the Police Relief Fund, and the Police Pension Fund.

The following is a statistical report of the activities of the bureau during the current year as compared with the previous year:

	Current Year	Previous Year
Memoranda of law prepared	68	83
Legal matters forwarded to Corporation Counsel	122	144
Letters requesting legal information	756	807
Letters requesting departmental records	139	111
Matters for publication	17	26
Court appearances of members of bureau	4,678	4,621
Conferences	94	103
Lectures at Police Academy	30	33
Reports on proposed legislation	194	255
Deciphering of codes	79	27
Expert testimony	31	16
Notices to court witnesses	55	81
Briefs prepared	22	18
Court papers prepared	258	-

13. One of the functions of the Legal Bureau is to   13.____

    A. review and make recommendations on proposed Federal laws affecting law enforcement
    B. prepare opinions on all measures introduced in the State Legislature and the City Council
    C. furnish the Police Department with pertinent information concerning all new Federal and State laws
    D. analyze all laws affecting the work of the Police Department

14. The one of the following that is NOT a function of the Legal Bureau is   14.____

    A. law enforcement and crime prevention
    B. prosecution of all cases in Women's Court
    C. advise and represent the Police Sports Association
    D. lecturing at the Police Academy

15. Members of the Legal Bureau frequently appear in Magistrate's Court for the purpose of   15.____

    A. defending members of the Police Force
    B. raising issues of importance to the Police Department
    C. prosecuting all offenders arrested by members of the Force
    D. facilitating proper determination of questions of law requiring technical presentation

16. The Legal Bureau sponsored a bill that would

    A. extend the licenses of gunsmiths
    B. prohibit the sale of switchblade knives to children of any size
    C. place confidence men and swindlers in the same category as jostlers in the Penal Law
    D. prohibit desk officers from admitting gamblers, confidence men, and swindlers to bail

16.____

17. From the report, it is NOT reasonable to infer that

    A. fewer bills affecting the Police Department were introduced in the current year
    B. the preparation of court papers was a new activity assumed in the current year
    C. the Code of Criminal Procedure authorizes desk officers to accept bail in certain cases
    D. the penalty for jostling and swindling is the same

17.____

18. According to the statistical report, the activity showing the GREATEST percentage of decrease in the current year as compared to the previous year was

    A. matters for publication
    B. reports on proposed legislation
    C. notices to court witnesses
    D. memoranda of law prepared

18.____

19. The State Legislature has declared it illegal

    A. to sell switchblade knives of any size to children under 16
    B. for an unauthorized person to sell or possess a hypodermic syringe or needle
    C. to extend the licensing period of gunsmiths
    D. for desk officers to take bail in gambling cases

19.____

20. According to the statistical report, the Legal Bureau, during the current year, as compared with the previous year, did NOT

    A. write more letters requesting departmental records and fewer letters requesting legal information
    B. prepare more briefs and fewer reports on proposed legislation
    C. prepare fewer court papers and more memoranda of law
    D. give fewer notices to court witnesses and decipher more codes

20.____

Questions 21-25.

DIRECTIONS: In answering Questions 21 through 25, the following definitions of crime should be applied, bearing in mind that ALL elements contained in the definition must be present in order to charge a person with that crime.

BURGLARY is the breaking and entering a building with intent to commit some crime therein.

EXTORTION is the obtaining of property from another, with his consent, induced by a wrongful use of force or fear, or under color of official right.

LARCENY is the taking and carrying away of the personal property of another with intent to deprive or defraud the owner of the use and benefit of such property.

ROBBERY is the unlawful taking of the personal property of another from his person or his presence, by force or violence or by putting him in fear of injury, immediate or future, to his person or property.

21. If A entered B's store during business hours, tied B to a chair and then helped himself to the contents of B's cash register, A, upon arrest, should be charged with 21._____

    A. burglary   B. extortion   C. larceny   D. robbery

22. If A broke the pane of glass in the window of B's store, stepped in and removed some merchandise from the window, he should, upon arrest, be charged with 22._____

    A. burglary   B. extortion   C. larceny   D. robbery

23. If A, after B had left for the day, found the door of B's store open, walked in, took some merchandise, and then left through the same open door, he should, upon arrest, be charged with 23._____

    A. burglary   B. extortion   C. larceny   D. robbery

24. If A, by threatening to report B for failure to pay to the city the full amount of sales tax he had collected from various customers, induced B to give him the contents of his cash register, A should, upon arrest, be charged with 24._____

    A. burglary   B. extortion   C. larceny   D. robbery

25. If A, on a crowded subway station, put his hand into B's pocket and removed B's wallet without his knowledge, A should, upon arrest, be charged with 25._____

    A. burglary   B. extortion   C. larceny   D. robbery

KEY (CORRECT ANSWERS)

1.	C		11.	C
2.	D		12.	B
3.	A		13.	D
4.	D		14.	A
5.	B		15.	D
6.	D		16.	C
7.	B		17.	D
8.	A		18.	A
9.	D		19.	B
10.	A		20.	C

21.	D
22.	A
23.	C
24.	B
25.	C

SCANNING MAPS

One section of the exam tests your ability to orient yourself within a given region on a map. Using the map accompanying questions 1 through 3; choose the best way of getting from one point to another.

The New Bridge is closed to traffic because it has a broken span.

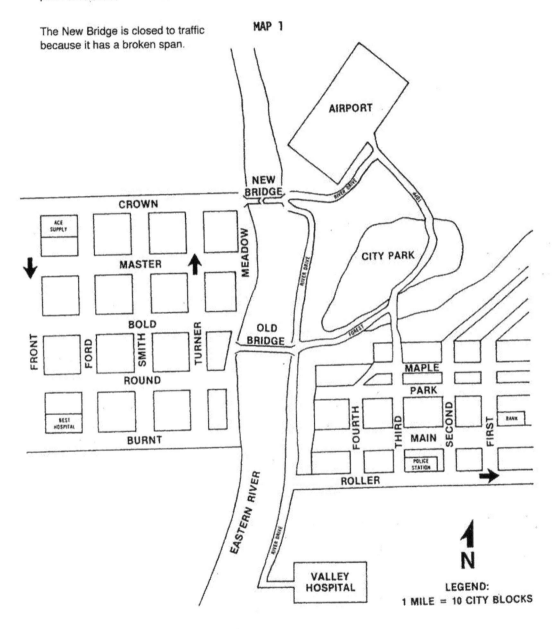

MAP 1

Arrows (━━➤) indicate on-way traffic and direction of traffic. A street marked by an arrow is one way for the entire length of the street.

SAMPLE QUESTIONS

1. Officers in a patrol car which is at the Airport receive a call for assistance at Best Hospital. The shortest route without breaking the law is:
   A. Southwest on River Drive, right on Forest, cross Old Bridge, south on Meadow, and west on Burnt to hospital entrance.
   B. Southwest on River Drive, right on New Bridge, left on Meadow, west on Burnt to hospital entrance.
   C. Southwest on River Drive, right on Old Bridge, left on Turner, right on Burnt to hospital entrance.
   D. North on River Drive to Topp, through City Park to Forest, cross Old Bridge, left on Meadow, west on Burnt to hospital entrance.

2. After returning to the police station, the officers receive a call to pick up injured persons at an accident site (located on the east side of New Bridge) and return to Valley Hospital. The shortest route without breaking the law is:

   A. West on Roller, north on River Drive, left to accident scene at New Bridge, then north on River Drive to hospital entrance.
   B. North on Third, left on Forest, north on River Drive, left to accident scene at new Bridge, then south on River Drive to hospital entrance.
   C. East on Roller, left on First, west on Maple, north on Third, left on Forest, north on River Drive to accident scene at New Bridge, then south on River Drive to hospital entrance.
   D. North on Third, left on Forest, cross Old Bridge, north on Meadow to New Bridge, south on Meadow, east over Old Bridge, then south on River Drive to hospital entrance.

3. While at the Valley Hospital, the officers receive a call asking them to pick up materials at the Ace Supply and return them to the police station. The shortest route without breaking the law is:
   A. North on River Drive, cross New Bridge, west on Crown to Ace Supply, then south on Front, east on Burnt, north on Meadow, cross Old Bridge, east on Forest, south on Third to police station.
   B. North on River Drive, right on Roller to police station, then north on Third, left on Forest, cross Old Bridge, north on Meadow, west on Crown to Ace Supply.
   C. North on River Drive, cross Old Bridge, north on Meadow, west on Crown to Ace Supply, then east on Crown, south on Meadow, cross Old Bridge, east on Forest, south on Third to police station.
   D. North on River Drive, cross Old Bridge, south on Meadow, west on Burnt, north on Front to Ace Supply, then east on Crown, south on Meadow, cross Old Bridge, east on Forest, south on Third to police station.

KEY (CORRECT ANSWERS)

1. A
2. B
3. C

72

VISUAL SCANNING

MAP READING

COMMENTARY

This is a test of your ability to orient yourself within a given section or neighborhood of a city or community. In each problem, you are in a vehicle, and you are to choose the shortest way to get from one location to another without breaking any laws. In order to solve each problem, you will need to study the map accompanying each set of four problems. Always begin with the first problem in the set. The starting point for the vehicle in the first problem will be marked by the symbol ➡. On the sample map below, the vehicle is heading east on Scott. You will be asked to find your way from the first location to the second location. Each location will be marked with an *X*. Some of the streets on the map are one-way streets. An arrow ⇨

shows the direction in which you may travel on a street. If there is no arrow, you may travel in either direction. These maps are NOT real. Do not confuse them with any area you may know. Below is a sample problem

SAMPLE QUESTION

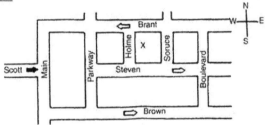

You are on Scott, and you are going to Holme. What is the MOST direct way to get there without breaking the law?
You are on Scott, and you are going to Holme. What is the MOST direct way to get there without breaking the law?

    A.   Go right on Main, left on Brown, left on Boulevard, left on Steven, right on Holme to telephone
    B.   Go left on Main, right on Brant, right on Holme to telephone
    C.   Go right on Main, left on Brown, left on Parkway, right on Steven, left on Holme to telephone
    D.   Go right on Main, left on Brown, left on Boulevard, left on Brant, left on Holme to telephone

The MOST direct way to get from the starting point to the location without breaking the law is described in choice C. Therefore, you would have marked C in the space at the right.

EXAMINATION SECTION
TEST 1

DIRECTIONS: Each map will be followed by several questions. For each question, you will be asked to go from one street to another street. There is ONLY ONE viable selection for each question, although it may not be the shortest route. Any street marked with either a ➡ or a ⬅ is a one-way street.
Unmarked streets are two-ways.
In some cases, a PARTICULAR location on a street is mentioned in the question. This information should be used in arriving at a correct answer. All maps are hypothetical. *PRINT THE LETTER OF THE CORRECT ANSWER IN THE SPACE AT THE RIGHT.*

Questions 1-5.

DIRECTIONS: For Questions 1 to 5, use the following map.

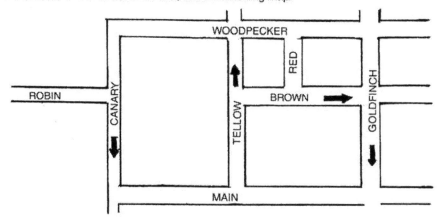

1. From Brown (east of Red) to Robin.

    A. Left on Goldfinch, left on Woodpecker, left on Canary, right on Robin
    B. Right on Goldfinch, right on Main, right on Yellow, left on Woodpecker, left on Canary, right on Robin
    C. Right on Goldfinch, right on Main, right on Canary, left on Robin
    D. Right on Goldfinch, left on Main, right on Canary, right on Robin

1.____

2. From Canary to Red.

    A. Left on Main, left on Goldfinch, left on Woodpecker, left on Red
    B. Left on Main, left on Yellow, left on Woodpecker, right on Red
    C. Left on Main, left on Yellow, right on Brown, left on Red
    D. Right on Main, left on Goldfinch, left on Brown, right on Red

2.____

3. From Woodpecker (west of Yellow) to Brown.

    3.____

    A. Left on Canary, left on Main, left on Yellow, right on Robin
    B. Right on Yellow, left on Brown
    C. Right on Yellow, left on Main, left on Goldfinch, right on Brown
    D. Right on Goldfinch, left on Brown

4. From Robin to Goldfinch.

    4.____

    A. Right on Canary, left on Main, left on Goldfinch
    B. Left on Canary, right on Woodpecker, right on Goldfinch
    C. Right on Canary, left on Main, left on Yellow, right on Brown, right on Goldfinch
    D. Right on Canary, left on Main, right on Yellow, left on Brown, left on Goldfinch

5. From Red to Main.

    5.____

    A. Left on Brown, left on Goldfinch, left on Main
    B. Right on Brown, right on Yellow, left on Woodpecker, right on Canary, left on Main
    C. Right on Brown, left on Yellow, right on Main
    D. Left on Brown, right on Goldfinch, right on Main

Questions 6-11.

DIRECTIONS: For Questions 6 to 11, use the following map.

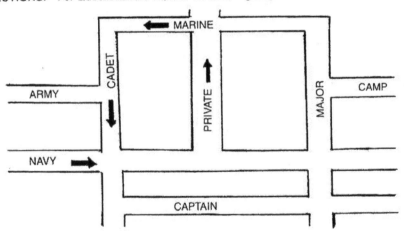

6. From Army to Camp.

    6.____

    A. Right on Cadet, left on Navy, right on Major, right on Camp
    B. Left on Cadet, left on Marine, right on Major, left on Camp
    C. Right on Cadet, left on Navy, left on Major, right on Camp
    D. Right on Cadet, right on Navy, left on Major, left on Camp

7. From Captain to Marine.

    7.____

    A. Left on Major, left on Marine
    B. Left on Major, left on Navy, right on Private, left on Marine

    C. Right on Cadet, right on Marine
    D. Right on Cadet, right on Navy, left on Private, left on Marine

8. From Navy (between Private and Major) to Cadet.

    A. Right on Major, right on Captain, right on Cadet
    B. Right on Private, left on Marine, right on Cadet
    C. Left on Major, left on Marine, left on Cadet
    D. Right on Captain, right on Navy, right on Cadet

8._____

9. From Navy (west of Cadet) to Array.

    A. Left on Private, left on Marine, left on Cadet, right on Army
    B. Left on Private, right on Marine, right on Army
    C. Left on Cadet, left on Army
    D. Right on Major, right on Captain, right on Cadet, left on Army

9._____

10. From Major to Army.

    A. Right on Navy, right on Cadet, right on Army
    B. Right on Captain, right on Cadet, left on Army
    C. Right on Navy, right on Private, left on Marine left on Cadet, right on Army
    D. Left on Marine, left on Cadet, right on Army

10._____

11. From Private to Captain.

    A. Right on Marine, right on Major, right on Captain
    B. Left on Navy, left on Major, right on Captain
    C. Left on Marine, left on Cadet, left on Captain
    D. Left on Marine, left on Cadet, left on Navy, left on Major, right on Captain

11._____

Questions 12-18.

DIRECTIONS: For Questions 12 to 18, use the following map.

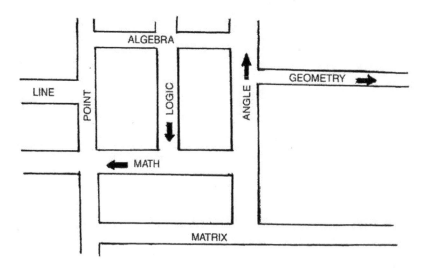

12. From Math to Angle (north of Algebra).   12._____

    A. Left on Point, right on Matrix, left on Angle
    B. Right on Point, right on Algebra, left on Angle
    C. Right on Logic, right on Algebra, left on Angle
    D. Left on Logic, left on Matrix, left on Angle

13. From Algebra to Geometry.   13._____

    A. Left on Logic, left on Math, right on Angle, right on Geometry
    B. Right on Point, left on Matrix, left on Angle, right on Geometry
    C. Left on Logic, right on Math, right on Point, right on Algebra, right on Angle, left on Geometry
    D. Left on Point, left on Matrix, left on Angle, right on Geometry

14. From Line to Logic.   14._____

    A. Left on Point, right on Algebra, right on Logic
    B. Right on Point, left on Math, left on Logic
    C. Left on Point, left on Algebra, right on Logic
    D. Right on Point, left on Matrix, right on Angle, left on Math, right on Logic

15. From Angle (between Math and Algebra) to Point.   15._____

    A. Left on Math, right on Point
    B. Left on Algebra, left on Point
    C. Left on Matrix, right on Point
    D. Left on Logic, right on Math, left on Point

16. From Matrix to Algebra.   16._____

    A. Right on Point, right on Math, left on Angle, left on Algebra
    B. Right on Angle, left on Algebra
    C. Right on Point, right on Algebra
    D. Left on Math, left on Point, right on Algebra

17. From Line to Geometry.   17._____

    A. Left on Point, right on Algebra, right on Angle, left on Geometry
    B. Right on Point, left on Math, left on Angle, right on Geometry
    C. Left on Point, left on Algebra, right on Logic, left on Angle, right on Geometry
    D. Right on Point, left on Matrix, left on Angle, right on Geometry

18. From Logic to Matrix.   18._____

    A. Right on Math, left on Point, left on Matrix
    B. Right on Math, right on Point, right on Matrix
    C. Left on Math, left on Angle, left on Matrix
    D. Right on Algebra, right on Angle, right on Matrix

Questions 19-25.

DIRECTIONS: For Questions 19 to 25, use the following map.

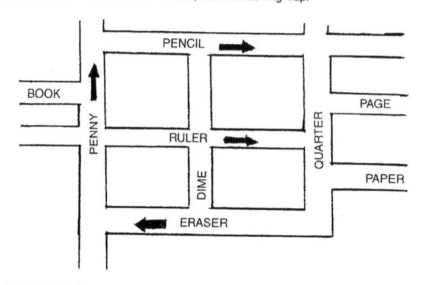

19.   From Page to Dime.

    A.   Right on Quarter, left on Pencil, left on Dime
    B.   Left on Quarter, right on Ruler, right on Dime
    C.   Right on Quarter, right on Pencil, left on Dime
    D.   Left on Quarter, right on Eraser, right on Dime

19.____

20.   From Penny to Eraser (between Dime and Quarter).

    A.   Right on Pencil, right on Quarter, right on Eraser
    B.   Right on Pencil, right on Dime, right on Eraser
    C.   Right on Ruler, left on Quarter, right on Eraser
    D.   Left on Ruler, right on Dime, right on Eraser

20.____

21.   From Book to Quarter (south of Paper).

    A.   Right on Penny, left on Ruler, right on Quarter
    B.   Left on Penny, right on Ruler, right on Quarter
    C.   Right on Penny, left on Eraser, left on Quarter
    D.   Left on Penny, right on Pencil, right on Quarter

21.____

22.   From Paper to Pencil (west of Dime).

    A.   Right on Quarter, left on Pencil
    B.   Left on Quarter, right on Eraser, right on Penny, right on Pencil
    C.   Right on Quarter, right on Eraser, right on Dime, right on Pencil
    D.   Left on Quarter, right on Eraser, right on Dime, left on Pencil

22.____

23. From Pencil (between Dime and Quarter) to Book.   23._____

    A. Right on Dime, right on Eraser, left on Penny, left on Book
    B. Right on Quarter, right on Ruler, right on Penny, left on Book
    C. Right on Quarter, right on Eraser, right on Penny, left on Book
    D. Right on Dime, right on Ruler, left on Book

24. From Penny (south of Eraser) to Dime (north of Ruler).   24._____

    A. Right on Ruler, left on Dime
    B. Right on Ruler, right on Dime
    C. Right on Pencil, left on Dime
    D. Right on Pencil, right on Quarter, right on Dime

25. From Ruler (west of Penny) to Paper.   25._____

    A. Right on Dime, left on Eraser, right on Paper
    B. Right on Quarter, left on Paper
    C. Left on Penny, right on Pencil, right on Quarter, right on Paper
    D. Right on Penny, left on Eraser, left on Quarter, right on Paper

---

KEY (CORRECT ANSWERS)

1.	B	11.	C
2.	C	12.	B
3.	A	13.	D
4.	C	14.	A
5.	D	15.	B
6.	C	16.	C
7.	A	17.	D
8.	C	18.	A
9.	A	19.	D
10.	D	20.	A

21.	D
22.	B
23.	C
24.	A
25.	B

79

TEST 2

DIRECTIONS: Each map will be followed by several questions. For each question, you will be asked to go from one street to another street. There is ONLY ONE viable selection for each question, although it may not be the shortest route. Any

street marked with either a ➡ or a ⬅ is a one-way street. Unmarked streets are two-ways.

In some cases, a PARTICULAR location on a street is mentioned in the question. This information should be used in arriving at a correct answer. All maps are hypothetical. *PRINT THE LETTER OF THE CORRECT ANSWER IN THE SPACE AT THE RIGHT.*

Questions 1-6.

DIRECTIONS: For Questions 1 to 6, use the following map.

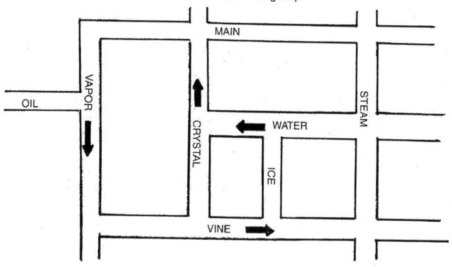

1. From Steam (north of Water) to Ice.   1.____

    A. Right on Water, left on Ice
    B. Right on Water, left on Crystal, left on Vine, left on Ice
    C. Left on Main, left on Crystal, right on Vine, right on Ice
    D. Left on Main, right on Vapor, left on Vine, right on Ice

2. From Oil to Main (east of Crystal).   2.____

    A. Right on Vapor, right on Crystal, left on Main
    B. Left on Vapor, right on Main
    C. Right on Vapor, left on Vine, left on Crystal, right on Main
    D. Left on Vapor, right on Vine, left on Main

3. From Water to Oil.   3.____

    A. Right on Crystal, left on Vapor, right on Oil
    B. Left on Crystal, right on Vine, right on Vapor, left on Oil
    C. Right on Crystal, left on Main, left on Vapor, right on Oil
    D. Left on Ice, right on Vapor, left on Oil

4. From Vine (between Crystal and Ice) to Crystal.   4.____

    A. Left on Ice, right on Steam, left on Crystal
    B. Left on Ice, left on Water, right on Crystal
    C. Left on Ice, right on Water, left on Crystal
    D. Left on Ice, left on Steam, right on Crystal

5. From Main (between Crystal and Steam) to Vine (east of Ice).   5.____

    A. Left on Crystal, left on Vine
    B. Right on Steam, right on Vine
    C. Right on Steam, right on Water, left on Ice, left on Vine
    D. Right on Steam, right on Water, right on Crystal, right on Vine

6. From Ice to Crystal (south of Water).   6.____

    A. Left on Water, left on Crystal
    B. Right on Water, left on Steam, left on Main, left on Crystal
    C. Right on Vine, right on Crystal
    D. Left on Water, right on Crystal, left on Main, left on Vapor, left on Vine, left oh Crystal

Questions 7-12.

DIRECTIONS: For Questions 7 to 12, use the following map.

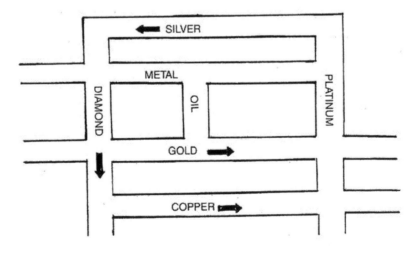

7. From Copper (west of Platinum) to Oil.   7.____

    A. Right on Diamond, right on Metal, right on Oil
    B. Left on Platinum, left on Gold, right on Oil
    C. Right on Diamond, right on Gold, left on Oil
    D. Left on Platinum, left on Metal, left on Oil

8. From Silver to Platinum (south of Copper).   8.____

    A. Left on Diamond, left on Gold, right on Platinum
    B. Left on Diamond, left on Copper, left on Platinum
    C. Right on Metal, left on Platinum
    D. Left on Diamond, left on Gold, left on Platinum

9. From Oil to Diamond (north of Metal).   9.____

    A. Left on Metal, left on Diamond
    B. Right on Gold, right on Diamond
    C. Left on Metal, right on Diamond
    D. Left on Gold, right on Copper, left on Diamond

10. From Platinum (between Gold and Copper) to Gold (between Oil and Diamond)   10.____

    A. Left on Metal, left on Oil, left on Gold
    B. Left on Silver, right on Diamond, right on Gold
    C. Left on Metal, left on Diamond, left on Gold
    D. Left on Silver, left on Oil, right on Gold

11. From Metal (west of Diamond) to Silver.   11.____

    A. Left on Diamond, right on Silver
    B. Left on Platinum, left on Silver
    C. Right on Platinum, right on Silver
    D. Right on Diamond, left on Silver

12. From Diamond (south of Copper) to Diamond (north of Metal).   12.____

    A. Right on Copper, left on Platinum, left on Silver, left on Diamond
    B. Right on Gold, left on Oil, left on Metal, left on Diamond
    C. Right on Copper, left on Platinum, left on Metal, right on Diamond
    D. Right on Copper, left on Platinum, left on Gold, right on Diamond

Questions 13-21.

DIRECTIONS: For Questions 13 to 21, use the following map.

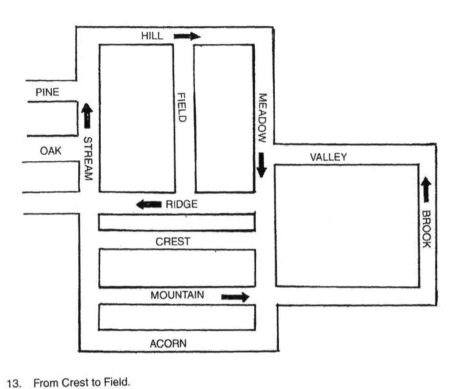

13. From Crest to Field.

    13.____

    A. Left on Meadow, left on Ridge, right on Field
    B. Right on Stream, right on Hill, left on Field
    C. Right on Meadow, right on Ridge, left on Field
    D. Right on Stream, right on Hill, right on Field

14. From Valley to Oak.

    14.____

    A. Left on Meadow, right on Mountain, left on Stream, left on Oak
    B. Left on Meadow, right on Ridge, right on Stream, left on Oak
    C. Right on Meadow, left on Hill, left on Stream, right on Oak
    D. Left on Meadow, left on Crest, right on Stream, left on Oak

15. From Field to Mountain (east of Meadow).

    15.____

    A. Right on Hill, right on Meadow, left on Mountain
    B. Right on Ridge, right on Stream, left on Mountain
    C. Left on Ridge, right on Meadow, right on Mountain
    D. Right on Hill, left on Stream, right on Mountain

16. From Pine to Ridge (east of Field).

    16.____

    A. Left on Stream, right on Hill, right on Field, right on Ridge
    B. Right on Stream, left on Ridge

    C.   Left on Stream, left on Field, left on Ridge
    D.   Left on Stream, right on Hill, right on Meadow, right on Ridge

17.   From Brook to Mountain (west of Meadow).   17._____

    A.   Left on Valley, left on Meadow, right on Acorn, right on Stream, right on Mountain
    B.   Left on Valley, left on Meadow, right on Mountain
    C.   Left on Valley, right on Meadow, right on Ridge, left on Stream, left on Mountain
    D.   Left on Meadow, right on Mountain

18.   From Acorn to Meadow (between Crest and Ridge).   18._____

    A.   Right on Stream, right on Mountain, left on Meadow
    B.   Left on Stream, left on Crest, right on Meadow
    C.   Right on Stream, right on Hill, right on Meadow
    D.   Right on Stream, right on Crest, right on Meadow

19.   From Ridge (east of Field) to Brook.   19._____

    A.   Right on Meadow, left on Mountain, left on Brook
    B.   Left on Stream, left on Crest, right on Meadow, left on Mountain, left on Brook
    C.   Left on Meadow, right on Valley, right on Brook
    D.   Right on Field, right on Hill, right on Meadow, left on Mountain, left on Brook

20.   From Meadow (between Crest and Mountain) to Oak.   20._____

    A.   Right on Acorn, right on Stream, left on Oak
    B.   Right on Crest, right on Stream, left on Oak
    C.   Right on Mountain, right on Stream, left on Oak
    D.   Left on Hill, left on Stream, right on Oak

21.   From Acorn to Ridge (west of Field).   21._____

    A.   Left on Meadow, left on Ridge
    B.   Right on Mountain, left on Brook, left on Valley, right on Meadow, left on Ridge
    C.   Right on Stream, right on Hill, right on Field, right on Ridge
    D.   Right on Stream, right on Mountain, left on Meadow, left on Ridge

Questions 22-25.

DIRECTIONS: For Questions 22 to 25, use the following map.

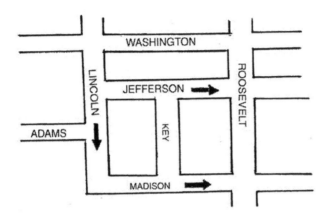

22. From Roosevelt (south of Madison) to Adams.   22.____

    A. Left on Washington, right on Lincoln, right on Adams
    B. Left on Jefferson, left on Lincoln, right on Adams
    C. Left on Washington, left on Lincoln, right on Adams
    D. Right on Jefferson, right on Key, right on Lincoln, left on Adams

23. From Madison (west of Key) to Jefferson (east of Roosevelt).   23.____

    A. Left on Roosevelt, left on Jefferson
    B. Left on Key, right on Jefferson
    C. Left on Key, left on Jefferson
    D. Left on Roosevelt, right on Washington, right on Jefferson

24. From Lincoln (south of Jefferson) to Adams.   24.____

    A. Right on Jefferson, right on Key, right on Madison, left on Adams
    B. Left on Jefferson, left on Lincoln, right on Adams
    C. Left on Washington, right on Lincoln, left on Adams
    D. Left on Madison, left on Roosevelt, left on Washington, left on Lincoln, right on Adams

25. From Washington (between Lincoln and Roosevelt) to Key.   25.____

    A. Right on Lincoln, left on Jefferson, right on Key
    B. Right on Roosevelt, right on Jefferson, left on Key
    C. Right on Roosevelt, right on Madison, right on Key
    D. Left on Lincoln, left on Madison, left on Key

KEY (CORRECT ANSWERS)

1.	A	11.	B
2.	C	12.	A
3.	C	13.	D
4.	B	14.	B
5.	C	15.	A
6.	D	16.	D
7.	D	17.	A
8.	A	18.	C
9.	C	19.	D
10.	C	20.	A

21.	C
22.	C
23.	B
24.	D
25.	D

MAP READING

EXAMINATION SECTION
TEST 1

DIRECTIONS: Each question or incomplete statement is followed by several suggested answers or completions. Select the one that BEST answers the question or completes the statement. *PRINT THE LETTER OF THE CORRECT ANSWER IN THE SPACE AT THE RIGHT.*

Questions 1-3.

DIRECTIONS: Questions 1 through 3 are to be answered SOLELY on the basis of the map which appears on the next page. The flow of traffic is indicated by the arrow. If there is only one arrow shown, then traffic flows only in the direction indicated by the arrow. If there are two arrows shown, then traffic flows in both directions. You must follow the flow of traffic.

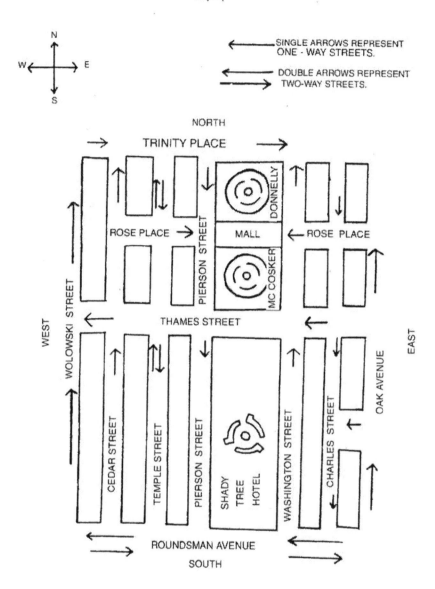

1. Police Officers Simms and O'Brien are located at Roundsman Avenue and Washington   1.____
    Street. The radio dispatcher has assigned them to investigate a motor vehicle accident at
    the corner of Pierson Street and Rose Place.
    Which one of the following is the SHORTEST route for them to take in their patrol car,
    making sure to obey all traffic regulations?
    Travel

    A. west on Roundsman Avenue, then north on Temple Street, then east on Thames
        Street, then north on Pierson Street to Rose Place
    B. east on Roundsman Avenue, then north on Oak Avenue, then west on Rose Place
        to Pierson Street
    C. west on Roundsman Avenue, then north on Temple Street, then east on Rose
        Place to Pierson Street
    D. east on Roundsman Avenue, then north on Oak Avenue, then west on Thames
        Street, then north on Temple Street, then east on Rose Place to Pierson Street

2. Police Officers Sears and Castro are located at Cedar Street and Roundsman Avenue.   2.____
    They are called to respond to the scene of a burglary at Rose Place and Charles Street.
    Which one of the following is the SHORTEST route for them to take in their patrol car,
    making sure to obey all traffic regulations?
    Travel

    A. east on Roundsman Avenue, then north on Oak Avenue, then west on Rose Place
        to Charles Street
    B. east on Roundsman Avenue, then north on Washington Street, then east on Rose
        Place to Charles Street
    C. west on Roundsman Avenue, then north on Wolowski Street, then east on Trinity
        Place, then south on Charles Street to Rose Place
    D. east on Roundsman Avenue, then north on Charles Street to Rose Place

3. Police Officer Glasser is in an unmarked car at the intersection of Rose Place and Tem-   3.____
    ple Street when he begins to follow two robbery suspects. The suspects go south for two
    blocks, then turn left for two blocks, then make another left turn for one more block. The
    suspects realize they are being followed and make a left turn and travel two more blocks
    and then make a right turn.
    In what direction are the suspects now headed?

    A. North   B. South   C. East   D. West

Questions 4-6.

DIRECTIONS: Questions 4 through 6 are to be answered SOLELY on the basis of the follow-
                ing map. The flow of traffic is indicated by the arrows. If there is only one arrow
                shown, then traffic flows only in the direction indicated by the arrow. If there are
                two arrows shown, then traffic flows in both directions. You must follow the flow
                of traffic.

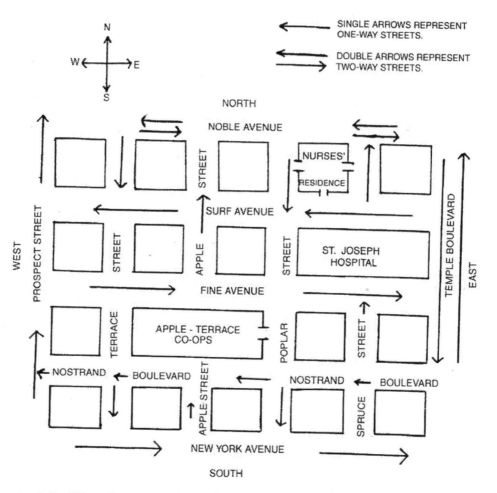

4. Police Officers Gannon and Vine are located at the intersection of Terrace Street and Surf Avenue when they receive a call from the radio dispatcher stating that they need to respond to an attempted murder at Spruce Street and Fine Avenue.
Which one of the following is the SHORTEST route for them to take in their patrol car, making sure to obey all traffic regulations?
Travel _____ to Spruce Street.

4. ____

    A.   west on Surf Avenue, then north on Prospect Street, then east on Noble Avenue, then south on Poplar Street, then east on Fine Avenue
    B.   east on Surf Avenue, then south on Poplar Street, then east on Fine Avenue
    C.   west on Surf Avenue, then south on Prospect Street, then east on Fine Avenue
    D.   south on Terrace Street, then east on Fine Avenue

5. Police Officers Sears and Ronald are at Nostrand Boulevard and Prospect Street. They receive a call assigning them to investigate a disruptive group of youths at Temple Boulevard and Surf Avenue.
Which one of the following is the SHORTEST route for them to take in their patrol car, making sure to obey all traffic regulations?
Travel

    A. north on Prospect Street, then east on Surf Avenue to Temple Boulevard
    B. north on Prospect Street, then east on Noble Avenue, then south on Temple Boulevard to Surf Avenue
    C. north on Prospect Street, then east on Fine Avenue, then north on Temple Boulevard to Surf Avenue
    D. south on Prospect Street, then east on New York Avenue, then north on Temple Boulevard to Surf Avenue

5.____

6. While on patrol at Prospect Street and New York Avenue, Police Officers Ross and Rock are called to a burglary in progress near the entrance to the Apple-Terrace Co-ops on Poplar Street midway between Fine Avenue and Nostrand Boulevard.
Which one of the following is the SHORTEST route for them to take in their patrol car, making sure to obey all traffic regulations?
Travel _____ Poplar Street.

    A. east on New York Avenue, then north
    B. north on Prospect Avenue, then east on Fine Avenue, then south
    C. north on Prospect Street, then east on Surf Avenue, then south
    D. east on New York Avenue, then north on Temple Boulevard, then west on Surf Avenue, then south

6.____

Questions 7-8.

DIRECTIONS: Questions 7 and 8 are to be answered SOLELY on the basis of the map which appears below. The flow of traffic is indicated by the arrows. If there is only one arrow shown, then traffic flows only in the direction indicated by the arrow. If there are two arrows shown, then traffic flows in both directions. You must follow the flow of traffic.

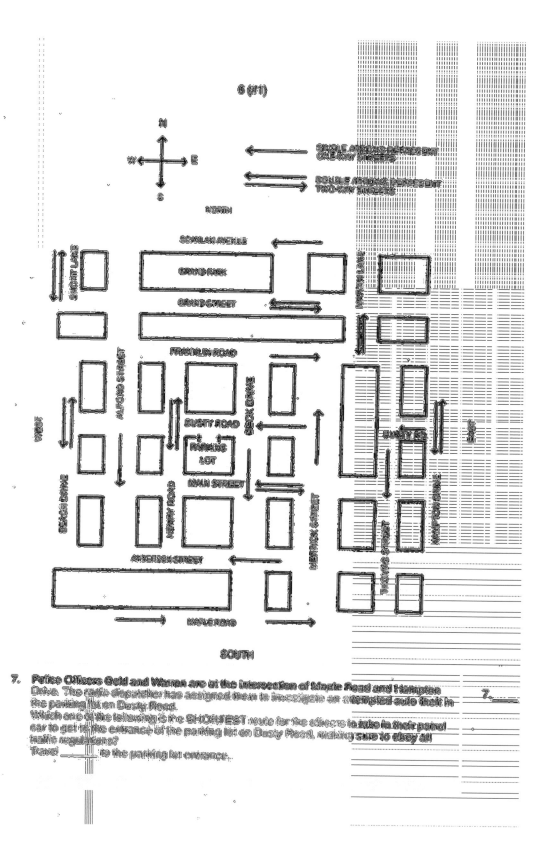

6 (#1)

SINGLE ARROWS REPRESENT ONE-WAY STREETS

DOUBLE ARROWS REPRESENT TWO-WAY STREETS

NORTH

SCHLAKI AVENUE

GRAND PARK

GRAND STREET

FRANKLIN ROAD

SHORT LANE

ALFORD STREET

BECK DRIVE

DUSTY ROAD

PARKING LOT

MAIN STREET

BEACH DRIVE

HENRY ROAD

MERRICK STREET

ANDERSON STREET

MAPLE ROAD

WEST

EAST

DUSTY ST.

HAMPTON DRIVE

THOMAS STREET

HORTON LANE

SOUTH

7. Police Officers Gold and Warren are at the intersection of Maple Road and Hampton Drive. The radio dispatcher has assigned them to investigate an attempted auto theft in the parking lot on Dusty Road.
Which one of the following is the SHORTEST route for the officers to take in their patrol car to get to the entrance of the parking lot on Dusty Road, making sure to obey all traffic regulations?
Travel _____ to the parking lot entrance.

7. _____

A. north on Hampton Drive, then west on Dusty Road
B. west on Maple Road, then north on Beck Drive, then west on Dusty Road
C. north on Hampton Drive, then west on Anderson Street, then north on Merrick Street, then west on Dusty Road
D. west on Maple Road, then north on Merrick Street, then west on Dusty Road

8. Police Officer Gladden is in a patrol car at the intersection of Beach Drive and Anderson Street when he spots a suspicious car. Police Officer Gladden calls the radio dispatcher to determine if the vehicle was stolen. Police Officer Gladden then follows the vehicle north on Beach Drive for three blocks, then turns right and proceeds for one block and makes another right. He then follows the vehicle for two blocks, and then they both make a left turn and continue driving. Police Officer Gladden now receives a call from the dispatcher stating the car was reported stolen and signals for the vehicle to pull to the side of the road.
In what direction was Police Officer Gladden heading at the time he signaled for the other car to pull over?

8.____

A. North   B. East   C. South   D. West

Questions 9-10.

DIRECTIONS: Questions 9 and 10 are to be answered SOLELY on the basis of the map which appears on the following page. The flow of traffic is indicated by the arrows. If there is only one arrow shown, then traffic flows only in the direction indicated by the arrow. If there are two arrows shown, then traffic flows in both directions. You must follow the flow of traffic.

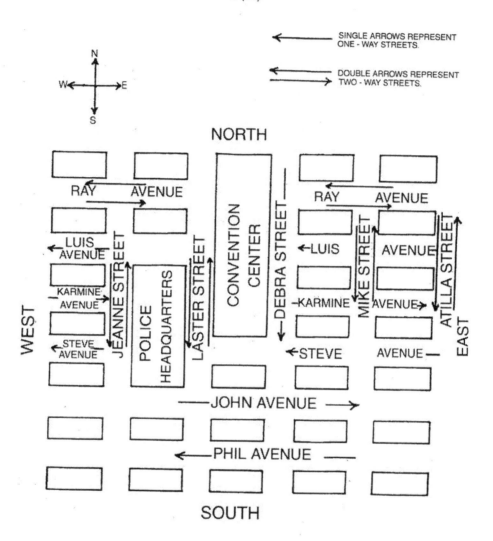

9. While in a patrol car located at Ray Avenue and Atilla Street, Police Officer Ashley receives a call from the dispatcher to respond to an assault at Jeanne Street and Karmine Avenue.
Which one of the following is the SHORTEST route for Officer Ashley to follow in his patrol car, making sure to obey all traffic regulations?
Travel

9.____

   A. south on Atilla Street, west on Luis Avenue, south on Debra Street, west on Steve Avenue, north on Lester Street, west on Luis Avenue, then one block south on Jeanne Street

   B. south on Atilla Street, then four blocks west on Phil Avenue, then north on Jeanne Street to Karmine Avenue

94

    C.   west on Ray Avenue to Debra Street, then five blocks south to Phil Avenue, then west to Jeanne Street, then three blocks north to Karmine Avenue

    D.   south on Atilla Street, then four blocks west on John Avenue, then north on Jeanne Street to Karmine Avenue

10.   After taking a complaint report from the assault victim, Officer Ashley receives a call from the dispatcher to respond to an auto larceny in progress at the corner of Debra Street and Luis Avenue.
Which one of the following is the SHORTEST route for Officer Ashley to follow in his patrol car, making sure to obey all traffic regulations?
Travel

10.____

    A.   south on Jeanne Street to John Avenue, then east three blocks on John Avenue, then north on Mike Street to Luis Avenue, then west to Debra Street

    B.   south on Jeanne Street to John Avenue, then east two blocks on John Avenue, then north on Debra Street to Luis Avenue

    C.   north on Jeanne Street two blocks, then east on Ray Avenue for one block, then south on Lester Street to Steve Avenue, then one block east on Steve Avenue, then north on Debra Street to Luis Avenue

    D.   south on Jeanne Street to John Avenue, then east on John Avenue to Atilla Street, then north three blocks to Luis Avenue, then west to Debra Street

Questions 11-13.

DIRECTIONS: Questions 11 through 13 are to be answered SOLELY on the basis of the following map. The flow of traffic is indicated by the arrows. You must follow the flow of traffic.

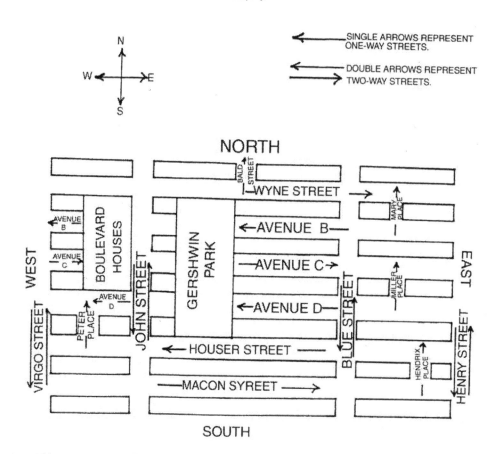

11. Police Officers Ranking and Fish are located at Wyne Street and John Street. The radio   11.___
dispatcher has assigned them to investigate a motor vehicle accident at the corner of
Henry Street and Houser Street.
Which one of the following is the SHORTEST route for them to take in their patrol car,
making sure to obey all traffic regulations?
Travel

    A.   four blocks south on John Street, then three blocks east on Houser Street to Henry
        Street

    B.   two blocks east on Wyne Street, then two blocks south on Blue Street, then two
        blocks east on Avenue C, then two blocks south on Henry Street

    C.   two blocks east on Wyne Street, then five blocks south on Blue Street, then two
        blocks east on Macon Street, then one block north on Henry Street

    D.   five blocks south on John Street, then three blocks east on Macon Street, then one
        block north to Houser Street

12. Police Officers Rizzo and Latimer are located at Avenue B and Virgo Street. They   12.____
respond to the scene of a robbery at Miller Place and Avenue D.
Which one of the following is the SHORTEST route for them to take in their patrol car,
making sure to obey all traffic regulations?
Travel _____ to Miller Place.

    A. one block north on Virgo Street, then four blocks east on Wyne Street, then three
blocks south on Henry Street, then one block west on Avenue D
    B. four blocks south on Virgo Street, then two blocks east on Macon Street, then two
blocks north on Blue Street, then one block east on Avenue D
    C. three blocks south on Virgo Street, then east on Houser Street to Henry Street,
then one block north on Henry Street, then one block west on Avenue D
    D. four blocks south on Virgo Street, then four blocks east to Henry Street, then north
to Avenue D, then one block west

13. Police Officer Bendix is in an unmarked patrol car at the intersection of John Street and   13.____
Macon Street when he begins to follow a robbery suspect. The suspect goes one block
east, turns left, travels for three blocks, and then turns right. He drives for two blocks and
then makes a right turn. In the middle of the block, the suspect realizes he is being followed and makes a u-turn. In what direction is the suspect now headed?

    A. North   B. South   C. East   D. West

Questions 14-15.

DIRECTIONS: Questions 14 and 15 are to be answered SOLELY on the basis of the following
map. The flow of traffic is indicated by the arrows. If there is only one arrow
shown, then traffic flows only in the direction indicated by the arrow. If there are
two arrows shown, then traffic flows in both directions. You must follow the flow
of traffic.

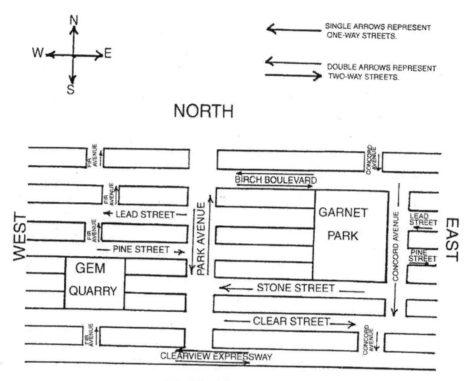

NORTH

SOUTH

14. You are located at Fir Avenue and Birch Boulevard and receive a request to respond to a
disturbance at Fir Avenue and Clear Street.
Which one of the following is the MOST direct route for you to take in your patrol car,
making sure to obey all traffic regulations?
Travel

   14._____

  A. one block east on Birch Boulevard, then four blocks south on Park Avenue, then
one block east on Clear Street
  B. two blocks east on Birch Boulevard, then three blocks south on Concord Avenue,
then two blocks west on Stone Street, then one block south on Park Avenue, then
one block west on Clear Street
  C. one block east on Birch Boulevard, then five blocks south on Park Avenue, then
one block west on the Clearview Expressway, then one block north on Fir Avenue
  D. two blocks south on Fir Avenue, then one block east on Pine Street, then three
blocks south on Park Avenue, then one block east on the Clearview Expressway,
then one block north on Fir Avenue

15. You are located at the Clearview Expressway and Concord Avenue and receive a call to respond to a crime in progress at Concord Avenue and Pine Street. Which one of the following is the MOST direct route for you to take in your patrol car, making sure to obey all traffic regulations?

    15.____

Travel

    A. two blocks west on the Clearview Expressway, then one block north on Fir Avenue, then one block east on Clear Street, then four blocks north on Park Avenue, then one block east on Birch Boulevard, then two blocks south on Concord Avenue

    B. one block north on Concord Avenue, then one block west on Clear Street, then one block north on Park Avenue, then one block east on Stone Street, then one block north on Concord Avenue

    C. one block west on the Clearview Expressway, then four blocks north on Park Avenue, then one block west on Lead Street, then one block south on Fir Avenue

    D. one block west on the Clearview Expressway, then five blocks north on Park Avenue, then one block east on Birch Boulevard, then two blocks south on Concord Avenue

Questions 16-20.

DIRECTIONS: Questions 16 through 20 are to be answered SOLELY on the basis of the following map. The flow of traffic is indicated by the arrows. You must follow the flow of traffic.

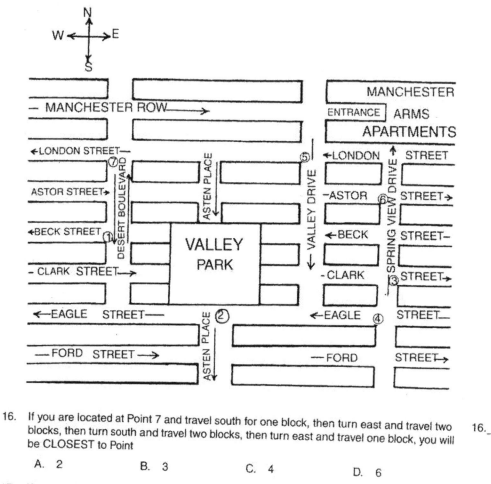

16. If you are located at Point 7 and travel south for one block, then turn east and travel two blocks, then turn south and travel two blocks, then turn east and travel one block, you will be CLOSEST to Point

    16.____

    A. 2   B. 3   C. 4   D. 6

17. If you are located at Point 3 and travel north for one block, and then turn west and travel one block, and then turn south and travel two blocks, and then turn west and travel one block, you will be CLOSEST to Point

    17.____

    A. 1   B. 2   C. 4   D. 6

18. You are located at Astor Street and Spring View Drive. You receive a call of a crime in progress at the intersection of Beck Street and Desert Boulevard.
Which one of the following is the MOST direct route for you to take in your patrol car, making sure to obey all traffic regulations?
Travel

    18.____

    A. one block north on Spring View Drive, then three blocks west on London Street, then two blocks south on Desert Boulevard
    B. three blocks west on Astor Street, then one block south on Desert Boulevard

C. one block south on Spring View Drive, then three blocks west on Beck Street
D. three blocks south on Spring View Drive, then three blocks west on Eagle Street, then two blocks north on Desert Boulevard

19. You are located on Clark Street and Desert Boulevard and must respond to a disturbance at Clark Street and Spring View Drive.
Which one of the following is the MOST direct route for you to take in your patrol car, making sure to obey all traffic regulations?
Travel

    19._____

A. two blocks north on Desert Boulevard, then three blocks east on Astor Street, then two blocks south on Spring View Drive
B. one block south on Desert Boulevard, then three blocks east on Eagle Street, then one block north on Spring View Drive
C. two blocks north on Desert Boulevard, then two blocks east on Astor Street, then three blocks south on Valley Drive, then one block east on Eagle Street, then one block north on Spring View Drive
D. two blocks north on Desert Boulevard, then two blocks east on Astor Street, then two blocks south on Valley Drive, then one block east on Clark Street

20. You are located at Valley Drive and Beck Street and receive a call to respond to the corner of Asten Place and Astor Street.
Which one of the following is the MOST direct route for you to take in your patrol car, making sure to obey all traffic regulations?
Travel _____ on Astor Street.

    20._____

A. one block north on Valley Drive, then one block west
B. two blocks south on Valley Drive, then one block east on Eagle Street, then three blocks north on Spring View Drive, then two blocks west
C. two blocks south on Valley Drive, then two blocks west on Eagle Street, then three blocks north on Desert Boulevard, then one block east
D. one block south on Valley Drive, then one block east on Clark Street, then two blocks north on Spring View Drive, then two blocks west

---

KEY (CORRECT ANSWERS)

1.	C		11.	B
2.	A		12.	A
3.	A		13.	A
4.	D		14.	C
5.	C		15.	D
6.	B		16.	B
7.	C		17.	B
8.	B		18.	A
9.	A		19.	D
10.	A		20.	C

CODING
EXAMINATION SECTION

COMMENTARY

An ingenious question-type called coding, involving elements of alphabetizing, filing, name and number comparison, and evaluative judgement and application, has currently won wide acceptance in testing circles for measuring clerical aptitude and general ability, particularly on the senior (middle) grades (levels).

While the directions for this question usually vary in detail, the candidate is generally asked to consider groups of names, codes, and numbers, and then, according to a given plan, to arrange codes in alphabetic order; to arrange these in numerical sequence; to re-arrange columns of names and numbers in correct order; to espy errors in coding; to choose the correct coding arrangement in consonance with the given directions and examples, etc.

This question-type appears to have few parameters in respect to form, substance, or degree of difficulty.

Accordingly acquaintance with, and practice in, the coding question is recommended for the serious candidate.

TEST 1

DIRECTIONS: Answer questions 1 through 8 an the basis of the code table and the instructions given below.

Code Letter for Traffic Problem	B	H	Q	J	F	L	M	I
Code Number for Action Taken	1	2	3	4	5	6	7	8

Assume that each of the capital letters on the above chart is a radio code for a particular traffic problem and that the number immediately below each capital letter is the radio code for the correct action to be taken to deal with the problem. For instance, "1" is the action to be taken to deal with problem "B", "2" is the action to be taken to deal with problem "H", and so forth.

In each question, a series of code letters is given in Column 1. Column 2 gives four different arrangements of code numbers. You are to pick the answer (A, B, C, or D) in Column 2 that gives the code numbers that match the code letters in the same order

SAMPLE QUESTION

Column 1		Column 2
BHLFMQ	A.	125678
	B.	216573
	C.	127653
	D.	126573

According to the chart, the code numbers that correspond to these code letters are as follows: B - 1, M - 2, L- 6, F - 5, M - 7, Q - 3. Therefore, the right answer is 126573. This answer is D in Column 2.

Column 1		Column 2	
1. BHQLMI		A. 123456	1.____
		B. 123567	
		C. 123678	
		D. 125678	
2. HBJQLF		A. 214365	2.____
		B. 213456	
		C. 213465	
		D. 214387	
3. QHMLFJ		A. 321654	3.____
		B. 345678	
		C. 327645	
		D. 327654	
4. FLQJIM		A. 543287	4.____
		B. 563487	
		C. 564378	
		D. 654378	
5. FBIHMJ		A. 518274	5.____
		B. 152874	
		C. 528164	
		D. 517842	
6. MIHFQB		A. 872341	6.____
		B. 782531	
		C. 782341	
		D. 783214	
7. JLFHQIM		A. 465237	7.____
		B. 456387	
		C. 4652387	
		D. 4562387	
8. LBJQIFH		A. 6143852	8.____
		B. 6134852	
		C. 61437852	
		D. 61431852	

KEY (CORRECT ANSWERS)

1.	C	5.	A
2.	A	6.	B
3.	D	7.	C
4.	B	8.	A

TEST 2

DIRECTIONS: Questions 1 through 5 are based on the following list showing the name and number of each of nine inmates.

1.	Johnson	4.	Thompson	7.	Gordon
2.	Smith	5.	Frank	8.	Porter
3.	Edwards	6.	Murray	9.	Lopez

Each question consists of 3 sets of numbers and letters. Each set should consist of the numbers of three inmates and the first letter of each of their names. The letters should be in the same order as the numbers. In at least two of the three choices, there will be an error. On your answer sheet, mark only that choice in which the letters correspond with the numbers and are in the same order. If all three sets are wrong, mark choice D in your answer space.

SAMPLE QUESTION
A. 386 EPM
B. 542 FST
C. 474 LGT

Since 3 corresponds to E for Edwards, 8 corresponds to P for Porter, and 6 corresponds to M for Murray, choice A is correct and should be entered in your answer space. Choice B is wrong because letters T and S have been reversed. Choice C is wrong because the first number, which is 4, does *NOT* correspond with the first letter of choice C, which is L. It should have been T. If choice A were also wrong, then D would be the correct answer.

1.	A.	382 EGS	B.	461 TMJ	C.	875 PLF	1.____
2.	A.	549 FLT	B.	692 MJS	C.	758 GSP	2.____
3.	A.	936 LEM	B.	253 FSE	C.	147 JTL	3.____
4.	A.	569 PML	B.	716 GJP	C.	842 PTS	4.____
5.	A.	356 FEM	B.	198 JPL	C.	637 MEG	5.____

Questions 6-10

DIRECTIONS: Answer questions 6 through 10 on the basis of the following information:

In order to make sure stock is properly located, incoming units are stored as follows:

STOCK NUMBERS			BIN NUMBERS	
00100	-	39999	D30,	L44
40000	-	69999	I4L,	D38
70000	-	99999	41L,	80D
100000 and over			614,	83D

Using the above table, choose the answer A, B, C, or D, which lists the correct Bin Number for the Stock Number given

6. 17243

    A. 41L   B. 83D   C. I4L   D. D30   6.____

7. 9219

    A. D38   B. L44   C. 614   D. 41L   7.____

8. 90125

    A. 41L   B. 614   C. D38   D. D30   8.____

9. 10001

    A. L44   B. D38   C. 80D   D. 83D   9.____

10. 200100

    A. 41L   B. I4L   C. 83D   D. D30   10.____

KEY (CORRECT ANSWERS)

1. B
2. D
3. A
4. C
5. C

6. D
7. B
8. A
9. A
10. C

TEST 3

DIRECTIONS: Assume that the Police Department is planning to conduct a statistical study of individuals who have been convicted of crimes during a certain year. For the purpose of this study, identification numbers are being assigned to individuals in the following manner:

The first two digits indicate the age of the individual:
The third digit indicates the sex of the individual:
1. male
2. female

The fourth digit indicates the type of crime involved:
1. criminal homicide
2. forcible rape
3. robbery
4. aggravated assault
5. burglary
6. larceny
7. auto theft
8. other

The fifth and sixth digits indicate the month in which the conviction occurred:
01. January
02. February, etc.

Answer questions 1 through 9 SOLELY on the basis of the above information and the following list of individuals and identification numbers.

Abbott, Richard	271304	Morris, Chris	212705
Collins, Terry	352111	Owens, William	231412
Elders, Edward	191207	Parker, Leonard	291807
George, Linda	182809	Robinson, Charles	311102
Hill, Leslie	251702	Sands, Jean	202610
Jones , Jackie	301106	Smith, Michael	421308
Lewis, Edith	402406	Turner, Donald	191601
Mack, Helen	332509	White, Barbara	242803

1. The number of women on the above list is

   A. 6   B. 7   C. 8   D. 9

2. The two convictions which occurred during February were for the crimes of

   A. aggravated assault and auto theft
   B. auto theft and criminal homicide
   C. burglary and larceny
   D. forcible rape and robbery

3. The ONLY man convicted of auto theft was

   A. Richard Abbott   B. Leslie Hill
   C. Chris Morris   D. Leonard Parker

1._____

2._____

3._____

4. The number of people on the list who were 25 years old or older is   4._____

    A. 6   B. 7   C. 8   D. 9

5. The *OLDEST* person on the list is   5._____

    A. Terry Collins   B. Edith Lewis
    C. Helen Mack   D. Michael Smith

6. The two people on the list who are the same age are   6._____

    A. Richard Abbott and Michael Smith
    B. Edward Elders and Donald Turner
    C. Linda George and Helen Mack
    D. Leslie Hill and Charles Robinson

7. A 28-year-old man who was convicted of aggravated assault in October would have identification number   7._____

    A. 281410   B. 281509   C. 282311   D. 282409

8. A 33-year-old woman convicted in April of criminal homicide would have identification number   8._____

    A. 331140   B. 331204   C. 332014   D. 332104

9. The number of people on the above list who were convicted during the first six months of the year is   9._____

    A. 6   B. 7   C. 8   D. 9

Questions 10-19.

DIRECTIONS: The following is a list of patients who were referred by various clinics to the laboratory for tests. After each name is a patient identification number. Answer questions 10 through 19 based on the information contained in this list and the explanation accompanying it.

The *first digit* refers to the clinic which made the referral:

    1. Cardiac   6. Hematology
    2. Renal   7. Gynecology
    3. Pediatrics   8. Neurology
    4. Opthalmology   9. Gastroenterology
    5. Orthopedics

The *second digit* refers to the sex of the patient:

    1. male   2. female

The *third* and *fourth digits* give the age of the patient.

The *last two digits give* the day of the month the laboratory tests were performed.

LABORATORY REFERRALS DURING JANUARY

Adams, Jacqueline	320917	Miller, Michael	511806
Black, Leslie	813406	Pratt, William	214411
Cook, Marie	511616	Rogers, Ellen	722428
Fisher, Pat	914625	Saunders, Sally	310229
Jackson, Lee	923212	Wilson, Jan	416715
James, Linda	624621	Wyatt, Mark	321326
Lane, Arthur	115702		

10. According to the list, the number of women referred to the laboratory during January was   10._____

    A. 4   B. 5   C. 6   D. 7

11. The clinic from which the MOST patients were referred was   11._____

    A. Cardiac   B. Gynecology
    C. Opthamology   D. Pediatrics

12. The YOUNGEST patient referred from any clinic other than Pediatrics was   12._____

    A. Leslie Black   B. Marie Cook
    C. Arthur Lane   D. Sally Saunders

13. The number of patients whose laboratory tests were performed on or before January 16 was   13._____

    A. 7   B. 8   C. 9   D. 10

14. The number of patients referred for laboratory tests who are under age 45 is   14._____

    A. 7   B. 8   C. 9   D. 10

15. The OLDEST patient referred to the clinic during January was   15._____

    A. Jacqueline Adams   B. Linda James
    C. Arthur Lane   D. Jan Wilson

16. The ONLY patient treated in the Orthopedics clinic was   16._____

    A. Marie Cook   B. Pat Fisher
    C. Ellen Rogers   D. Jan Wilson

17. A woman, age 37, was referred from the Hematology clinic to the laboratory. Her laboratory tests were performed on January 9. Her identification number would be   17._____

    A. 610937   B. 623709   C. 613790   D. 623790

18. A man was referred for lab tests from the Orthopedics clinic. He is 30 years old and his tests were performed on January 6. His identification number would be   18._____

    A. 413006   B. 510360   C. 513006   D. 513060

19. A 4 year old boy was referred from Pediatrics clinic to have laboratory tests on January 23. His identification number was   19._____

    A. 310422   B. 310423   C. 310433   D. 320403

KEY (CORRECT ANSWERS)

1.	B		11.	D
2.	B		12.	B
3.	B		13.	A
4.	D		14.	C
5.	D		15.	D
6.	B		16.	A
7.	A		17.	B
8.	D		18.	C
9.	C		19.	B
10.	B			

TEST 4

DIRECTIONS: Questions 1 through 10 are to be answered on the basis of the information and directions given on the following page.

Assume that you are a Senior Stenographer assigned to the personnel bureau of a city agency. Your supervisor has asked you to classify the employees in your agency into the following five groups:

A. employees who are college graduates, who are at least 35 years of age but less than 50, and who have been employed by the. city for five years or more;

B. employees who have been employed by the City for less than five years, who are not college graduates, and who earn at least $32,500 a year but less than $34,500;

C. employees who have been city employees for five years or more, who are at least 21 years of age but less than 35, and who are not college graduates;

D. employees who earn at least $34,500 a year but less than $36,000 who are college graduates, and who have been employed by the city for less than five years;

E. employees who are not included in any of the foregoing groups.

NOTE: In classifying these employees you are to compute age and period of service as of January 1, 2003. In all cases, it is to be assumed that each employee has been employed continuously in City service. In each question, consider only the information which will assist you in classifying each employee. Any information which is of no assistance in classifying an employee should not be considered.

SAMPLE: Mr. Brown, a 29-year-old veteran, was appointed to his present position of Clerk on June 1, 2000. He has completed two years of college. His present salary is $33,050.

The correct answer to this sample is B, since the employee has been employed by the city for less than five years, is not a college graduate, and earns at least $32,500 a year but less than $34,500 .

DIRECTIONS: Questions 1 to 10 contain excerpts from the personnel records of 10 employees in the agency. In the correspondingly numbered space on the right print the capital letter preceding the appropriate group into which you would place each employee,

1. Mr. James has been employed by the city since 1993, when he was graduated from a local college. Now 35 years of age, he earns $36,000 a year.

1.____

2. Mr. Worth began working in city service early in 1999. He was awarded his college degree in 1994, at the age of 21.
As a result of a recent promotion, he now earns $34,500 a year.

2.____

3. Miss Thomas has been a City employee since August 1, 1998. Her salary is $34,500 a year. Miss Thomas, who is 25 years old, has had only three years of high school training.

3.____

4. Mr. Williams has had three promotions since entering city service on January 1, 1991. He was graduated from college with honors in 1974, when he was 20 years of age. His present salary is $37,000 a year.

4.____

5. Miss Jones left college after two years of study to take an appointment to a position in the city service paying $33,300 a year. She began work on March 1, 1997 when she was 19 years of age.   5.____

6. Mr. Smith was graduated from an engineering college with honors in January 1998 and became a city employee three months later. His present yearly salary is $35,810 . Mr. Smith was born in 1976.   6.____

7. Miss Earnest was born on May 31, 1979. Her education consisted of four years of high school and one year of business school. She was appointed as a typist in a city agency on June 1, 1997. Her annual salary is $33,500.   7.____

8. Mr. Adams, a 24-year-old clerk, began his city service on July 1, 1999, soon after being discharged from the U.S.
    Army. A college graduate, his present annual salary is $33,200   8.____

9. Miss Charles attends college in the evenings, hoping to obtain her degree in 2004, when she will be 30 years of age. She has been a city employee since April 1998,and earns $33,350.   9.____

10. Mr. Dolan was just promoted to his present position after six years of city service. He was graduated from high school in 1982, when he was 18 years of age, but did not go on to college, Mr. Dolan's present salary is $33,500.   10.____

KEY (CORRECT ANSWERS)

1. A
2. D
3. E
4. A
5. C

6. D
7. C
8. E
9. B
10. E

TEST 5

DIRECTIONS: Questions 1 through 4 each contain five numbers that should be arranged in numerical order. The number with the lowest numerical value should be first and the number with the highest numerical value should be last. Pick that option which indicates the *correct* order of the numbers.

Examples:
A.	9;	18;	14;	15;	27
B.	9;	14;	15;	18;	27
C.	14;	15;	18;	27;	9
D.	9;	14;	15;	27;	18

The correct answer is B, which indicates the proper arrangement of the five numbers.

1. A. 20573; 20753; 20738; 20837; 20098
    B. 20098; 20753; 20573; 20738; 20837
    C. 20098; 20573; 20753; 20837; 20738
    D. 20098; 20573; 20738; 20753; 20837

1.____

2. A. 113492; 113429; 111314; 113114; 131413
    B. 111314; 113114; 113429; 113492; 131413
    C. 111314; 113429; 113492; 113114; 131413
    D. 111314; 113114; 131413; 113429; 113492

2.____

3. A. 1029763; 1030421; 1035681; 1036928; 1067391
    B. 1030421; 1029763; 1035681; 1067391; 1036928
    C. 1030421; 1035681; 1036928; 1067391; 1029763
    D. 1029763; 1039421; 1035681; 1067391; 1036928

3.____

4. A. 1112315; 1112326; 1112337; 1112349; 1112306
    B. 1112306; 1112315; 1112337; 1112326; 1112349
    C. 1112306; 1112315; 1112326; 1112337; 1112349
    D. 1112306; 1112326; 1112315; 1112337; 1112349

4.____

KEY (CORRECT ANSWERS)

1. D
2. B
3. A
4. C

TEST 6

DIRECTIONS: The phonetic filing system is a method of filing names in which the alphabet is
reduced to key code letters. The six key letters and their equivalents are as follows:

KEY LETTERS	EQUIVALENTS
b	p, f, v
c	s, k, g, j , q, x, z
d	t
l	none
m	n
r	none

A key letter represents itself.
Vowels (a, e, i, o and u) and the letters w, h, and y are omitted.
For example, the name GILMAN would be represented as follows:
   G is represented by the key letter C.
   I is a vowel and is omitted.
   L is a key letter and represents itself.
   M is a key letter and represents itself.
   A is a vowel and is omitted.
   N is represented by the key letter M.

Therefore, the phonetic filing code for the name GILMAN is CLMM.
Answer questions 1 through 10 based on the information on the previous page.

1.   The phonetic filing code for the name FITZGERALD would be   1.____
    A.   BDCCRLD   B.   BDCRLD   C.   BDZCRLD   D.   BTZCRLD

2.   The phonetic filing code CLBR may represent any one of the following names EXCEPT   2.____
    A.   Calprey   B.   Flower   C.   Glover   D.   Silver

3.   The phonetic filing code LDM may represent any one of the following names EXCEPT   3.____
    A.   Halden   B.   Hilton   C.   Walton   D.   Wilson

4.   The phonetic filing code for the name RODRIGUEZ would be   4.____
    A.   RDRC   B.   RDRCC   C.   RDRCZ   D.   RTRCC

5.   The phonetic filing code for the name MAXWELL would be   5.____
    A.   MCLL   B.   MCWL   C.   MCWLL   D.   MXLL

6.   The phonetic filing code for the name ANDERSON would be   6.____
    A.   AMDRCM   B.   ENDRSM   C.   MDRCM   D.   NDERCN

7.   The phonetic filing code for the name SAVITSKY would be   7.____
    A.   CBDCC   B.   CBDCY   C.   SBDCC   D.   SVDCC

8. The phonetic filing code CMC may represent any one of the following names EXCEPT   8.____

   A. James   B. Jayes   C. Johns   D. Jones

9. The *ONLY* one of the following names that could be represented by the phonetic filing code CDDDM would be   9.____

   A. Catalano   B. Chesterton   C. Cittadino   D. Cuttlerman

10. The *ONLY* one of the following names that could be represented by the phonetic filing code LLMCM would be   10.____

   A. Ellington   B. Hallerman   C. Inslerman   D. Willingham

---

KEY (CORRECT ANSWERS)

1. A
2. B
3. D
4. B
5. A

6. C
7. A
8. B
9. C
10. D

NAME AND NUMBER CHECKING
EXAMINATION SECTION
TEST 1

DIRECTIONS: Each question or incomplete statement is followed by several suggested answers or completions. Select the one that *BEST* answers the question or completes the statement. *PRINT THE LETTER OF THE CORRECT ANSWER IN THE SPACE AT THE RIGHT.*

Questions 1-10

DIRECTIONS: Questions 1 through 10 below present the identification numbers, initials, and last names of employees enrolled in a city retirement system. You are to choose the option (A, B, C, or D) that has the *identical* identification number, initials, and last name as those given in each question.

SAMPLE QUESTION

B145698 JL Jones
 A. B146798 JL Jones   B. B145698 JL Jonas
 C. P145698 JL Jones   D. B145698 JL Jones

The correct answer is D. Only option D shows the identification number, initials and last name exactly as they are in the sample question. Options A, B, and C have errors in the identification number or last name.

1. J297483 PL Robinson   1.____

  A. J294783 PL Robinson   B. J297483 PL Robinson
  C. J297483 PI Robinson   D. J297843 PL Robinson

2. S497662 JG Schwartz   2.____

  A. S497662 JG Schwarz   B. S497762 JG Schwartz
  C. S497662 JG Schwartz   D. S497663 JG Schwartz

3. G696436 LN Alberton   3.____

  A. G696436 LM Alberton   B. G696436 LN Albertson
  C. G696346 LN Albertson   D. G696436 LN Alberton

4. R774923 AD Aldrich   4.____

  A. R774923 AD Aldrich   B. R744923 AD Aldrich
  C. R774932 AP Aldrich   D. R774932 AD Allrich

5. N239638 RP Hrynyk   5.____

  A. N236938 PR Hrynyk   B. N236938 RP Hrynyk
  C. N239638 PR Hrynyk   D. N239638 RP Hrynyk

6. R156949 LT Carlson   6.____

  A. R156949 LT Carlton   B. R156494 LT Carlson
  C. R159649 LT Carlton   D. R156949 LT Carlson

7. T524697 MN Orenstein

    A. T524697 MN Orenstein   B. T524967 MN Orinstein
    C. T524697 NM Ornstein   D. T524967 NM Orenstein

7.____

8. L346239 JD Remsen

    A. L346239 JD Remson   B. L364239 JD Remsen
    C. L346329 JD Remsen   D. L346239 JD Remsen

8.____

9. P966438 SB Rieperson

    A. P996438 SB Reiperson   B. P966438 SB Reiperson
    C. R996438 SB Rieperson   D. P966438 SB Rieperson

9.____

10. D749382 CD Thompson

    A. P749382 CD Thompson   B. D749832 CD Thomsonn
    C. D749382 CD Thompson   D. D749823 CD Thomspon

10.____

Questions 11 - 20

DIRECTIONS: Each of Questions 11 through 20 gives the identification number and name of a person who has received treatment at a certain hospital. You are to choose the option (A, B, C, or D) which has *EXACTLY* the same identification number and name as those given in the question.

SAMPLE QUESTION

123765 Frank Y. Jones

    A. 123675 Frank Y. Jones
    B. 123765 Frank T. Jones
    C. 123765 Frank Y. Johns
    D. 123765 Frank Y. Jones

The correct answer is D. Only option D shows the identification number and name exactly as they are in the sample question. Option A has a mistake in the identification number. Option B has a mistake in the middle initial of the name. Option C has a mistake in the last name.

Now answer Questions 11 through 20 in the same manner.

11. 754898 Diane Malloy

    A. 745898 Diane Malloy
    B. 754898 Dion Malloy
    C. 754898 Diane Malloy
    D. 754898 Diane Maloy

11.____

12. 661818 Ferdinand Figueroa

    A. 661818 Ferdinand Figueroa
    B. 661618 Ferdinand Figueroa
    C. 661818 Ferdnand Figueroa
    D. 661818 Ferdinand Figueroa

12.____

13. 100101 Norman D. Braustein

    A. 100101 Norman D. Braustein
    B. 101001 Norman D. Braustein
    C. 100101 Norman P. Braustien
    D. 100101 Norman D. Bruastein

13.____

14. 838696 Robert Kittredge

    A. 838969 Robert Kittredge   14._____
    B. 838696 Robert Kittredge
    C. 388696 Robert Kittredge
    D. 838696 Robert Kittridge

15. 243716 Abraham Soletsky

    A. 243716 Abrahm Soletsky   15._____
    B. 243716 Abraham Solestky
    C. 243176 Abraham Soletsky
    D. 243716 Abraham Soletsky

16. 981121 Phillip M. Maas

    A. 981121 Phillip M. Mass   16._____
    B. 981211 Phillip M. Maas
    C. 981121 Phillip M. Maas
    D. 981121 Phillip N. Maas

17. 786556 George Macalusso

    A. 785656 George Macalusso   17._____
    B. 786556 George Macalusso
    C. 786556 George Maculasso
    D. 786556 George Macluasso

18. 639472 Eugene Weber

    A. 639472 Eugene Weber   18._____
    B. 639472 Eugene Webre
    C. 693472 Eugene Weber
    D. 639742 Eugene Weber

19. 724936 John J. Lomonaco

    A. 724936 John J. Lomanoco   19._____
    B. 724396 John J. Lomonaco
    C. 724936 John J. Lomonaco
    D. 724936 John J. Lamonaco

20. 899868 Michael Schnitzer

    A. 899868 Micheal Schnitzer   20._____
    B. 898968 Michael Schnizter
    C. 899688 Michael Schnitzer
    D. 899868 Michael Schnitzer

Questions: 21 - 28

DIRECTIONS: Questions 21 through 28 consist of lines of names, dates, and numbers which represent the names. membership dates, social security numbers, and members of the retirement system.For each question you are to choose the option (A, B, C, or D) in Column II which *EXACTLY* matches the information in Column I.

SAMPLE QUESTION

Column I

Crossen 12/23/56 173568929 253492

Column II

    A. Crossen 2/23/56 173568929
       253492
    B. Crossen 12/23/56 173568729
       253492
    C. Crossen 12/23/56 173568929
       253492
    D. Crossan 12/23/56 173568929
       258492

The correct answer is C. Only option C shows the name, date, and numbers exactly as they are in Column I. Option A has a mistake in the date. Option B has a mistake in the social security number. Option D has a mistake in the name and in the membership number.

21. Figueroa 1/15/64 119295386 147563

21._____

A.	Figueroa	1/5/64	119295386	147563
B.	Figueroa	1/15/64	119295386	147563
C.	Figueroa	1/15/64	119295836	147563
D.	Figueroa	1/15/64	119295886	147563

22. Goodridge 6/19/59 106237869 128352

22._____

A.	Goodridge	6/19/59	106287869	128332
B.	Goodrigde	6/19/59	106237869	128352
C.	Goodridge	6/9/59	106237869	128352
D.	Goodridge	6/19/59	106237869	128352

23. Balsam 9/13/57 109652382 116938

23._____

A.	Balsan	9/13/57	109652382	116938
B.	Balsam	9/13/57	109652382	116938
C.	Balsom	9/13/57	109652382	116938
D.	Balsalm	9/13/57	109652382	116938

24. Mackenzie 2/16/49 127362513 101917

24._____

A.	Makenzie	2/16/49	127362513	101917
B.	Mackenzie	2/16/49	127362513	101917
C.	Mackenzie	2/16/49	127362513	101977
D.	Mackenzie	2/16/49	127862513	101917

25. Halpern 12/2/73 115206359 286070

25._____

A.	Halpern	12/2/73	115206359	286070
B.	Halpern	12/2/73	113206359	286070
C.	Halpern	12/2/73	115206359	206870
D.	Halpern	12/2/73	115206359	286870

26. Phillips 4/8/66 137125516 192612

26._____

A.	Phillips	4/8/66	137125516	196212
B.	Philipps	4/8/66	137125516	192612
C.	Phillips	4/8/66	137125516	192612
D.	Phillips	4/8/66	137122516	192612

27. Francisce 11/9/63 123926037 152210

27._____

A.	Francisce	11/9/63	123826837	152210
B.	Francisce	11/9/63	123926037	152210
C.	Francisce	11/9/63	123936037	152210
D.	Franscice	11/9/63	123926037	152210

28. Silbert 7/28/54 118421999 178514

28.____

A.	Silbert	7/28/54	118421999	178544
B.	Silbert	7/28/54	184421999	178514
C.	Silbert	7/28/54	118421999	178514
D.	Siblert	7/28/54	118421999	178514

KEY (CORRECT ANSWERS)

1.	B		16.	C
2.	C		17.	B
3.	D		18.	A
4.	A		19.	C
5.	D		20.	D
6.	D		21.	B
7.	A		22.	D
8.	D		23.	B
9.	D		24.	B
10.	C		25.	A
11.	C		26.	C
12.	D		27.	B
13.	A		28.	C
14.	B			
15.	D			

TEST 2

Questions 1-3

DIRECTIONS: Items 1 to 3 are a test of your proofreading ability. Each item consists of Copy I and Copy II. You are to assume that Copy I in each item is correct. Copy II, which is meant to be a duplicate of Copy I, may contain some typographical errors. In each item, compare Copy II with Copy I and determine the number of errors in Copy II. If there are:

no errors, mark your answer A;
1 or 2 errors, mark your answer B;
3 or 4 errors, mark your answer C;
5 or 6 errors, mark your answer D;
7 errors or more, mark your answer E.

1.

1._____

COPY I
The Commissioner, before issuing any such license, shall cause an investigation to be made of the premises named and described in such application, to determine whether all the provisions of the sanitary code, building code, state industrial code, state minimum wage law, local laws, regulations of municipal agencies, and other requirements of this article are fully observed. (Section B32-169.0 of Article 23.)

COPY II
The Commissioner, before issuing any such license shall cause an investigation to be made of the premises named and described in such applecation, to determine whether all the provisions of the sanitary code, bilding code, state industrial code, state minimum wage laws, local laws, regulations of municipal agencies, and other requirements of this article are fully observed. (Section E32-169.0 of Article 23.)

2.

2._____

COPY I
Among the persons who have been appointed to various agencies are John Queen, 9 West 55th Street, Brooklyn; Joseph Blount, 2497 Durward Road, Bronx: Lawrence K. Eberhardt, 3194 Bedford Street, Manhattan; Reginald L. Darcy, 1476 Allerton Drive, Bronx; and Benjamin Ledwith, 177 Greene Street, Manhattan.

COPY II
Among the persons who have been appointed to various agencies are John Queen, 9 West 56th Street, Brooklyn, Joseph Blount, 2497 Dureward Road, Bronx: Lawrence K. Eberhart , 3194 Belford Street, Manhattan; Reginald L. Barcey, 1476 Allerton drive, Bronx; and Benjamin Ledwith, 177 Green Street, Manhattan.

3.

3._____

COPY I
Except as hereinafter provided, it shall be unlawful to use, store or have on hand any inflammable motion picture film in quantities greater than one standard or two sub-standard reels, or aggregating more than two thousand feet in length, or more than ten pounds in weight without the permit required by this section.

COPY II

Except as herinafter provided, it shall be unlawfull to use, store or have on hand any inflamable motion picture film, in quantities greater than one standard or two substandard reels or aggregating more than two thousand feet in length, or more then ten pounds in weight without the permit required by this section.

Questions 4-6

Questions 4 to 6 are a test of your proofreading ability. Each question consists of Copy I and Copy II. You are to assume that Copy I in each question is correct. Copy II, which is meant to be a duplicate of Copy I, may contain some typographical errors. In each question, compare Copy II with Copy I and determine the number of errors in Copy II. If there are

no errors, mark your answer A;
1 or 2 errors, mark your answer B;
3 or 4 errors, mark your answer C;
5 errors or more, mark your answer D.

4.   4.____

COPY I

It shall be unlawful to install wires or appliances for electric light, heat or power, operating at a potential in excess of seven hundred fifty volts, in or on any part of a building, with the exception of a central station, sub-station, transformer, or switching vault, or motor room; provided, however, that the Commissioner may authorize the use of radio transmitting apparatus under special conditions.

COPY II

It shall be unlawful to install wires or appliances for electric light, heat or power, operating at a potential in excess of seven hundred fifty volts, in or on any part of a building, with the exception of a central station, sub-station, transformer, or switching vault, or motor room, provided, however, that the Commissioner may authorize the use of radio transmitting apperatus under special conditions.

5.   5.____

COPY I

The grand total debt service for the fiscal year 2006-07 amounts to $350,563,718.63, as compared with $309,561,347.27 for the current fiscal year, or an increase of $41,002,371.36. The amount payable from other sources in 2006-07 shows an increase of $13,264,165.47, resulting in an increase of $27,733,205.89 payable from tax levy funds.

COPY II

The grand total debt service for the fiscal year 2006-07 amounts to $350,568,718.63, as compared with $309,561,347.27 for the current fiscel year, or an increase of $41,002,371.36. The amount payable from other sources in 2006-07 show an increase of $13,264,165.47 resulting in an increase of $27,733,295.89 payable from tax levy funds.

6.   6. ____

<u>COPY I</u>

The following site proposed for the new building is approximately rectangular in shape and comprises an entire block, having frontages of about 721 feet on 16th Road, 200 feet on 157th Street, 721 feet on 17th Avenue and 200 feet on 154th Street, with a gross area of about 144,350 square feet. The 2006-07 assessed valuation is $28,700,000 of which $6,000,000 is for improvements.

<u>COPY II</u>

The following site proposed for the new building is approximately rectangular in shape and comprises an entire block, having frontage of about 721 feet on 16th Road, 200 feet on 157th Street, 721 feet on 17th Avenue, and 200 feet on 134th Street, with a gross area of about 114,350 square feet. The 2006-07 assessed valuation is $28,700,000 of which $6,000,000 is for improvements.

———

KEY (CORRECT ANSWERS)

1. D
2. E
3. E
4. B
5. D
6. C

———

TEST 3

Questions 1-8

DIRECTIONS: Each of the Questions numbered 1 through 8 consists of three sets of names and name codes. In each question, the two names and name codes on the same line are supposed to be exactly the same.

Look carefully at each set of names and codes and mark your answer

    A.   if there are mistakes in all three sets
    B.   if there are mistakes in two of the sets
    C.   if there is a mistake in only one set
    D.   if there are no mistakes in any of the sets

SAMPLE QUESTION

The following sample question is given to help you understand the procedure

Macabe, John N. - V 53162	Macade, John N. - V 53162
Howard, Joan S. - J 24791	Howard, Joan S. - J 24791
Ware, Susan B. - A 45068	Ware, Susan B. - A 45968

In the above sample question, the names and name codes of the first set are not exactly the same because of the spelling of the last name (Macabe - Macade). The names and name codes of the second set are exactly the same. The names and name codes of the third set are not exactly the same because the two name codes are different (A 45068 - A 45968). Since there are mistakes in only 2 of the sets, the answer to the sample question is B.

1.   Powell, Michael C. - 78537 F   Powell, Michael C. - 78537 F   1.____
      Martinez, Pablo J. - 24435 P   Martinez, Pablo J. - 24435 P
      MacBane, Eliot M. - 98674 E   MacBane, Eliot M. - 98674 E

2.   Fitz-Kramer Machines Inc.   Fitz-Kramer Machines Inc.   2.____
            - 259090   - 259090
      Marvel Cleaning Service   Marvel Cleaning Service
            - 482657   - 482657
      Donato, Carl G. - 637418   Danato, Carl G. - 687418

3.   Martin Davison Trading Corp.   Martin Davidson Trading Corp.   3.____
            - 43108 T   - 43108 T
      Cotwald Lighting Fixtures   Cotwald Lighting Fixtures
            - 76065 L   - 70056 L
      R. Crawford Plumbers   R. Crawford Plumbers
            - 23157 C   - 23157 G

4.   Fraiman Engineering Corp.   Friaman Engineering Corp.   4._____
           - M4773   - M4773
      Neuman, Walter B. - N7745   Neumen, Walter B. - N7745
      Pierce, Eric M.   - W6304   Pierce, Eric M.   - W6304

5.   Constable, Eugene - B 64837   Comstable, Eugene - B 64837   5._____
      Derrick, Paul - H 27119   Derrik, Paul - H 27119
      Heller, Karen - S 49606   Heller, Karen - S 46906

6.   Hernando Delivery Service Co.   Hernando Delivery Service Co.   6._____
           - D 7456   - D 7456
      Barettz Electrical Supplies   Barettz Electrical Supplies
           - N 5392   - N 5392
      Tanner, Abraham - M 4798   Tanner, Abraham - M 4798

7.   Kalin Associates - R 38641   Kaline Associates - R 38641   7._____
      Sealey, Robert E. - P 63533   Sealey, Robert E. - P 63553
      Seals! Office Furniture   Seals! Office Furniture
           - R36742   - R36742

8.   Janowsky, Philip M.- 742213   Janowsky, Philip M.- 742213   8._____
      Hansen, Thomas H. - 934816   Hanson, Thomas H. - 934816
      L. Lester and Son Inc.   L. Lester and Son Inc.
           - 294568   - 294568

Questions 9-13

DIRECTIONS: Each of the questions number 9 through 13 consists of three sets of names
               and building codes. In each question, the two names and building codes on
               the same line are supposed to be exactly the same.

If you find an error or errors on only *one* of the sets in the question, mark your answer A; any
two of the sets in the question, mark your answer B; all *three* of the sets in the question, mark
your answer C; *none* of the sets in the question, mark your answer D.

Column I   Column II
Duvivier, Anne P. - X52714   Duviver, Anne P. - X52714
Dyrborg, Alfred - B4217   Dyrborg, Alfred - B4267
Dymnick, JoAnne - P482596   Dymnick, JoAnne - P482596

In the above sample question, the first set of names and building codes is not exactly the same
because the last names are spelled differently (Duvivier - Duviver). The second set of names
and building codes is not exactly the same because the building codes are different (B4217 -
B4267). The third set of names and building codes is exactly the same. Since there are mistakes in two of the sets of names and building codes, the answer to the sample question is B.

Now answer the questions on the following page using, the same procedure.

Column I	Column II	
9. Lautmann, Gerald G. - C2483 Lawlor, Michael - W44639 Lawrence, John J. - H1358	Lautmann, Gerald C. - C2483 Lawler, Michael - W44639 Lawrence, John J. - H1358	9.____
10. Mittmann, Howard - J4113 Mitchell, William T.- M75271 Milan, T. Thomas - Q67533	Mittmann, Howard - J4113 Mitchell, William T.- M75271 Milan, T. Thomas - Q67553	10.____
11. Quarles, Vincent - J34760 Quinn, Alan N. - S38813 Quinones, Peter W. - B87467	Quarles, Vincent - J34760 Quinn, Alan N. - S38813 Quinones, Peter W. - B87467	11.____
12. Daniels, Harold H. - A26554 Dantzler, Richard - C35780 Davidson, Martina - E62901	Daniels, Harold H - A26544 Dantzler, Richard - 035780 Davidson, Martin - E62901	12.____
13. Graham, Cecil J. - I20244 Granger, Deborah - T86211 Grant, Charles L. - G5788	Graham, Cecil J. - I20244 Granger, Deborah - T86211 Grant, Charles L. - G5788	13.____

KEY (CORRECT ANSWERS)

1.	D	8.	C
2.	C	9.	B
3.	A	10.	A
4.	B	11.	D
5.	A	12.	C
6.	D	13.	D
7.	B		

TEST 4

DIRECTIONS: In questions 1 to 10 there are five pairs of numbers or letters and numbers.
Compare each pair and decide how many pairs are *EXACTLY ALIKE. PRINT
THE LETTER OF THE CORRECT ANSWER IN THE SPACE AT THE RIGHT.*
- A. if only one pair is exactly alike
- B. if only two pairs are exactly alike
- C. if only three pairs are exactly alike
- D. if only four pairs are exactly alike
- E. if all five pairs are exactly alike

1. 73-F......F-73
    F-7373....F-7373
    F-733.....337-F

    FF-73. . . .FF-73
    373-FF...337-FF

    1._____

2. 0-17158. . ..0-17158
    0-11758....0-11758
    0-51178....0-51178

    0-71518 ... 0-71518
    0-15817... 0-15817

    2._____

3. 1A-7908....1A-7908
    7A-891.....7A-891
    9A-7018....9A-7081

    7A-8901....7A-8091
    1A-9078....1A-9708.

    3._____

4. 2V-6426....2V-6246
    2V-6426....2N-6426
    2V-6462....2V-6462

    2N-6246....2N-6246
    2N-6624....2N-6624

    4._____

5. 3NY-56......3ny-65
    6NY-3566....3ny-3566
    3NY-5663....5ny-3663

    5NY-356.....3NY-356
    5NY-6536....5NY-6536

    5._____

6. COB-065....COB-065
    LBC-650....LBC-650
    CDB-056....COB-065

    BCL-506....BCL-506
    DLB-560....DLB-560

    6._____

7. 4KQ-9130....4KQ-9130
    4KQ-9031....4KQ-9031
    4KQ-9013....4KQ-9013

    4KQ-9310....4KQ-9130
    4KQ-9301....4KQ-9301

    7._____

8. MK-89......MK-98
    MSK-998........MSK-998
    SMK-899....SMK-899

    98-MK......89-MK
    MOSK.......MOKS

    8._____

9. 8MD-2104....SMD-2014
    814-MD......814-MD
    MD-281......MD-481

    2MD-8140....2MD-8140
    4MD-8201. . . .4MD-8201

    9._____

10. 161-035. .. .161-035
     315-160....315-160
     165-301....165-301

     150-316.... 150-316
     131-650....131-650

     10._____

KEY (CORRECT ANSWERS)

1.	B	6.	D
2.	E	7.	D
3.	B	8.	B
4.	C	9.	C
5.	A	10.	E

———

TEST 5

DIRECTIONS: Each question or incomplete statement is followed by several suggested answers or completions. Select the one that *BEST* answers the question or completes the statement. *PRINT THE LETTER OF THE CORRECT ANSWER IN THE SPACE AT THE RIGHT.*

Questions 1-5

DIRECTIONS: Questions 1 through 5, inclusive, consist of groups of four displays representing license identification plates. Examine each group of plates and determine the number of plates in each group which are identical. Mark your answer sheets as follows:

If only two plates are identical, mark answer A.
If only three plates are identical, mark answer B.
If all four plates are identical, mark answer C.
If the plates are all different, mark answer D

EXAMPLE

ABC123	BCD123	ABC123	BCD235

Since only two plates are identical, the first and the third, the correct answer is A.

1.	PBV839	PVB839	PVB839	PVB839	1._____
2.	WTX083	WTX083	WTX083	WTX083	2._____
3.	B73609	D73906	BD7396	BD7906	3._____
4.	AK7423	AK7423	AK1423	A81324	4._____
5.	583Y10	683Y10	583Y01	583Y10	5._____

Questions 6-10

DIRECTIONS: Questions 6 through 10 consist of groups of numbers and letters similar to those which might appear on license plates. Each group of numbers and letters will be called a license identification. Choose the license identification lettered A, B, C, or D that *EXACTLY* matches the license identification shown next to the question number.

SAMPLE
NY 1977
ABC-123

| A. NY 1976 | B. NY 1977 | C. NY 1977 | D. NY 1977 |
| ABC-123 | ABC-132 | CBA-123 | ABC-123 |

The license identification given is NY 1977. The only choice
ABC-123.
that exactly matches it is the license identification next to the letter D. The correct answer is therefore D.

6.   NY 1976   6._____
                                      QLT-781

| A. NJ 1976 | B. NY 1975 | C. NY 1976 | D. NY 1977 |
| QLT-781 | QLT-781 | QLT-781 | QLT-781 |

7.   FLA 1977   7._____
                                      2-7LT58J

| A. FLA 1977 | B. FLA 1977 | C. FLA 1977 | D. LA 1977 |
| 2-7TL58J | 2-7LTJ58 | 2-7LT58J | 2-7LT58J |

8.   NY 1975   8._____
                                      OQC383

| A. NY 1975 | B. NY 1975 | C. NY 1975 | D. NY 1977 |
| OQC383 | OQC833 | QCQ383 | OCQ383 |

9.   MASS 1977   9._____
                                      B-8DK02

| A. MISS 1977 | B. MASS 1977 | C. MASS 1976 | D. MASS 1977 |
| B-8DK02 | B-8DK02 | B-8DK02 | B-80KD2 |

10.   NY 1976   10._____
                                      ZV0586

| A. NY 1976 | B. NY 1977 | C. NY 1976 | D. NY 1976 |
| 2V0586 | ZV0586 | ZV0586 | ZU0586 |

KEY (CORRECT ANSWERS)

1.	B	6.	C
2.	C	7.	C
3.	D	8.	A
4.	A	9.	B
5.	A	10.	C

TEST 6

DIRECTIONS: Assume that each of the capital letters in the table below represents the name of an employee enrolled in the city employees' retirement system. The number directly beneath the letter represents the agency for which the employee works, and the small letter directly beneath represents the code for the employee's account.

Name of Employee	L	O	T	Q	A	M	R	N	C
Agency	3	4	5	9	8	7	2	1	6
Account Code	r	f	b	i	d	t	g	e	n

In each of the following questions 1 through 3, the agency code numbers and the account code letters in Columns 2 and 3 should correspond to the capital letters in Column 1 and should be in the same consecutive order. For each question, look at each column carefully and mark your answer as follows:

If there are one or more errors *in Column 2 only* , mark your answer A.
If there are one or more errors *in Column 3 only*, mark your answer B.
If there are one or more errors in Column 2 and one or more errors in Column 3, mark your answer C.
If there are NO errors in either column, mark your answer D.
The following sample question is given to help you understand the procedure.

Column I	Column 2	Column 3
TQLMOC	583746	birtfn

In Column 2, the second agency code number (corresponding to letter Q) should be "9", not "8". Column 3 is coded correctly to Column 1. Since there is an error only in Column 2, the correct answer is A.

	Column 1	Column 2	Column 3	
1.	QLNRCA	931268	iregnd	1._____
2.	NRMOTC	127546	egftbn	2._____
3.	RCTALM	265837	gndbrt	3._____

KEY (CORRECT ANSWERS)

1. D
2. C
3. B

POLICE SCIENCE NOTES

POLICE COMMUNICATIONS

Communication can be defined as the transfer of information from one person to another. It can be accomplished in a variety of ways including the spoken word, written message, signal or electrical device. Geographically, communication involves the transmission of messages from one point to another, either interdepartmentally or intradepartmentally. Any exchange of words, messages, or signals in connection with police action may be classified as police communications.

History

Police communications, contrary to many modern beliefs, are as old as the police service itself. In 17th century England, policemen carried bells or lanterns for identification and as signal devices to give warnings or to summon assistance. The 18th century saw little improvement in police signaling equipment. Police officers in the 19th century utilized whistles, night sticks, and even their pistols as signal devices. The 20th century brought the introduction of electrical devices to the field of police communications. The horn, bell, light, telegraph, telephone, radio-telegraph, radio, radar, and now television, afford communications with infinitely increased efficiency. These developments also have produced great strides in the area of speed, range, and area coverage.

Along with these developments in the technical aspects of police communications, the written reporting system of law enforcement agencies have become considerably more sophisticated with the use of automatic and electronic data storage and processing equipment becoming more and more common. This progress has resulted in more accurate, complete, and easily recoverable information for police use.

The rapid growth of police communication probably is the best indication of its success in police administration. It has enabled a remarkable increase in the promptness and effectiveness of police action, especially in emergencies where time is of utmost importance, and closer and more effective control over patrolmen in the field. Most recently developed and available are: two-way radios small enough to be carried on an officer's belt; printout or screen display devices mounted in patrol cars with computer inquiry capability; and automatic query/response devices which show dispatchers or supervisors the geographic locations of patrol cars by radio direction finding systems. Advances in radio communication render perhaps the most important innovations in police methods since the introduction of fingerprinting.

Present Practice

Today's tools of communication are allowing police departments, both large and small, to increase the extent and efficiency of their service. Hardly a single police action is taken that does not involve some sort of communication. Original complaints are usually made to the police department by use of citizen-placed telephone calls. The information is relayed to police dispatchers or other appropriate personnel by use of interoffice phones or by use of mechanical devices, such as the pneumatic tube. In many cases two-way radio is used to relay information to patrol vehicles or to other police departments.

Also helping to stretch the police potential are systems of communication involving teletype, radiotelegraph, land-wire telegraph, long-distance phone circuits, interconnected computer and photo transmitting machines.

These are but a sample of what make up the network of communication found in most police departments. These tools plus proper techniques are invaluable in accomplishing the necessary steps to deal with natural disasters or nuclear attacks. Therefore, knowledge of such tools and techniques are imperative to successful actions of local police auxiliary units.

Telephone Procedures

The citizen's first contact with the police department is often a telephone conversation with an officer. On the telephone you are the police department's voice and whatever you say and how you say it creates for the citizen an impression of the department to that citizen. Every time you pick up the phone you are doing a public relations job. It may be good, bad, or indifferent. Why not always try for the good public relations job?

When considering proper procedures for the use of the telephone, courtesy and consideration are always the keywords. Even when receiving calls from persons who are agitated or excited the proper action remains much the same as in normal telephone calls. Since a large part of police telephone work is receiving calls the following procedures are essential ones.

1. Identify yourself immediately after answering.
2. Speak courteously.
3. Have pad and pencil handy-makes notes when necessary.

On the other hand, when *you* make a call follow the same basic guides of courtesy and consideration. This may be stated as follows:

1. Have in mind what you wish to know or say when your call is answered.
2. Identify yourself and state your business.
3. Have pad and pencil available-make notes when necessary.

Reaching for a telephone is one of our most frequent and familiar gestures. However, this does not guarantee good telephone usage. Proper procedures can result in good telephone usage and are important to proper police work.

Radio Procedure

Two-way radio might well be considered the backbone of police communications. In many instances the proper use of this instrument may well mean the difference between success or failure in any given situation. In general, the same guides apply as did to good telephone procedures, namely, courtesy and consideration. However, a few specific guides are identified for your use.

To transmit a message:

1. Be certain the dispatcher is not busy transmitting other messages.
2. Contact dispatcher, giving your identification, and then wait for dispatcher to answer.
3. Begin your message after the dispatcher has answered you.

While transmitting a message:

1. Speak distinctly into the microphone as in ordinary conversation. Too loud a voice distorts the reception.
2. Speak slowly.
3. Keep messages brief.
4. Mentally rehearse your message before transmitting.
5. Never use vulgar language.

The final rule cannot be overemphasized. Not only is such language in poor taste, but is prohibited by regulations of the FCC. Furthermore, any excess language used, and vulgar language is excess, may well confuse or distort the meaning of your message.

In learning to use radio communications effectively it is necessary to master the codes and specific procedures in effect in your local police department. Appendix II gives some samples of such procedures.

Emergency Information Media

In addition to the telephone and radio communications of the police service, during a CD emergency the auxiliary policeman will need to receive and act on messages disseminated by public information media (radio and television broadcasts, newspapers, etc.) as part of the emergency information program. Although these messages will be intended for the general public, they will also convey information of value to the auxiliary policeman in the performance of his duties. For example, in many local civil defense plans provision is made for certain radio stations to remain on the air as part of the Emergency Broadcasting System, and their broadcasts will convey official information on such matters as warning conditions and last-minute instructions regarding movement to shelters or relocation areas.

TELEMETRY AND COMMUNICATIONS

TABLE OF CONTENTS

Page

Unit 1. Emergency Medical Services Communication System   1

Phases of an Emergency Medical Services Communication System   1
System Components   3
Radio Communications: Voice and Telemetry   4

Unit 2: Communications Regulations and Procedures   7

Federal Communications Commission   7
Protocols and Communication Procedures   7
Dispatch Procedures   7
Relaying Information to the Physician   11
Techniques   12

Glossary   14

TELEMETRY AND COMMUNICATIONS

Unit 1. Emergency Medical Services Communication System

An emergency medical services (EMS) communication system helps coordinate all groups and persons involved in emergency response and care. Such a communication system should be able to coordinate emergency medical services and resources during major emergencies and disasters, as well as during individual emergencies.

Phases of an Emergency Medical Services Communication System

Access and notification. How to notify the system when an emergency has occurred is an important aspect of EMS communications. Although telephones are the most common means of access available to the public, their usefulness is limited by their number and location and by the public's confusion as to whom to call for emergency assistance. The Yellow Pages of the telephone directory may offer a wide choice of emergency ambulance services; and, furthermore, operators may be unprepared to accept and refer a true emergency call.

The telephone is most useful in an emergency when the 911 universal access number is available. A bystander then can dial 911 from a home telephone or a callbox without needing correct change to notify the dispatch agency. The call goes to a communications coordination center (CCC) for police, fire, and medical emergencies. The emergency services operator in the center then notifies the appropriate emergency service.

Some communities also have free telephones or callboxes available on the highways for emergency use. When these highway phones or callboxes are properly connected for prompt access to an emergency services center, they make it easier for citizens to obtain emergency services.

The notification phase of emergency medical communications can be improved through public education. The public should know when emergency care is needed, whom to call to obtain appropriate aid, what to say in order to obtain advice, and what to expect in the way of a response.

Dispatch. Once the system has been notified, there must be a process through which appropriate emergency vehicles are selected and directed to the scene of the illness or injury. Vehicles can be dispatched by telephone (hard-line communication), radio, or a combination telephone/radio connection (phone patch).

It is easier and more economical to coordinate emergency services if the CCC dispatches police, fire, and emergency medical vehicles. Such centers can be organized to cover county or other regional areas, depending on local policy and municipal preferences. The CCC is especially helpful in coordinating emergency services during major emergencies and disasters.

Communication between dispatcher and emergency personnel. The Emergency Medical Technician-Paramedic (EMT-P) must have use of a radio at all times: en route to the emergency scene, at the scene, during transport to the hospital, and while returning to base after completing a call. The capability for rapid interconnection to medical advice should be at the fingertips of the dispatcher.

Dispatcher-to-paramedic communication is important for several reasons. It enables the dispatcher to give the EMT-P additional information while en route. It lets the dispatcher know where the emergency vehicle is and about how long it will be busy. It also allows redirection of the vehicle either when en route to the original destination or when traveling to the base station after completing a call. Further, it allows the EMT-P to request police or fire department assistance, additional ambulances, or additional emergency medical personnel.

Three-way communication among the paramedic physician and emergency department. Physicians, although usually hospital based, may be linked to the ambulance by a communication system in their cars, homes, or offices so that they can order advanced life-support procedures at the scene and during transport. In some States, specially trained nurses, operating under standing orders from physicians, can provide this consultation link with EMT-P's.

Communication with emergency department personnel allows the EMT-P to report the patient's condition and expected arrival time. This procedure gives the emergency department time to assemble necessary equipment and prepare for specific problems. In addition, such communication allows redirection of the EMS team to another facility if the original one does not have adequate treatment capabilities or bed space for a particular case.

Paramedics often use two-way radios to communicate with the physician, nurse, and emergency department. By means of the communication patching capabilities at the base station, the ambulance en route can communicate by mobile radio via phone patch or cross-frequency radio patch to someone at the accident scene. In addition, the ambulance en route or at the scene can communicate by mobile radio via patch to a physician at home or in a vehicle equipped with a telephone or citizens band (CB) radio.

Portable radio transmitter/receivers can be used for communications between the emergency scene and the hospital physician, usually via the ambulance relay. In this way, the EMT-P can receive instructions at the scene without having to return to the vehicle to use the mobile transmitter/receiver.

Communication among area hospitals. In a mass casualty situation, communication among area hospitals may be necessary to request blood or special supplies. In this phase, communication among hospitals may be by radio, telephone, or radio-telephone combination.

Communication links with support agencies. Communication with such support agencies as the fire and police departments and civil defense office or with crisis intervention teams can be accomplished through CCC's or through separate dispatch centers.

Although it is possible for dispatch centers to communicate by telephone, such connections may be disrupted or overloaded during a disaster. Therefore, dedicated telephone lines (lines used exclusively between two points) and/or a backup radio network should be available.

Coordination of other radio networks to be used in contingency planning. Private communication systems that normally are available during disasters include the. following:
- The Amateur Radio Public Service Corps (ARPSC) (Contact the ARPSC at the American Radio Relay League, Inc., Newington, Conn. 06111, for information on specific area groups.)

- The Radio Amateur Civil Emergency Service (RACES) (Contact local civil defense officials for information on community resources.)
- Business and municipal radio service systems (e.g., taxi-dispatching and trucking services)
- CB highway safety groups, such as REACT and NEAR (Some have been specially organized to respond to emergency situations through Channel 9, a designated emergency channel.

System Components

The hardware (components) used for medical communications varies considerably from system to system. A description of some of the coon hardware components of a communication network follows.

Base station transmitters and receivers. The base station is used for dispatch and coordination and, ideally, should be in contact with all other elements of the system. Directional antennas should be placed in the proper position to serve the desired area for radio coverage and at the same time not interfere with bordering service areas. The highest point is not necessarily the best location. Wire connections from base radio units to the dispatch center may be the most desirable method for reducing the number of airwave (radio) transmissions. This method allows greater use of radio channels and precludes interference to neighboring services. Transmission levels are limited by the Federal Communications Commission (FCC). The minimum usable levels for signal reception are limited by manmade noise such as automobile ignitions. A good antenna system can compensate partially for these limitations.

Base stations with multiple channels to provide automatic rotation to an open channel are available.

Mobile transmitter/receivers. Mobile transmitter/receivers are mounted in the emergency vehicles. They come in different power ranges. The antenna system, the power range of the transmitter/receiver, the kinds of buildings in the area, and terrain features determine the distance over which the units can transmit a signal. The reliability and radio transmission range can be insured substantially if the network of base stations and telephone interconnections is properly engineered.

Portable transmitter/receivers (two-way portable radios). Portable transmitter/receivers are handheld so that they can be carried outside the emergency vehicle by the EMT-P. Medical control physicians also carry portable transmitter/receivers for use when they cannot be reached immediately via the hospital-circuit radio.

Portable units usually have a power limitation of 5 watts. The signal of a handheld transmitter can be boosted to equal the range of a mobile unit by retransmission through the vehicle or base station for network connection. Portable transmitter/receivers can transmit and receive multiple frequencies.

Repeaters. Essentially repeaters are miniature base stations used to extend the transmitting and receiving range of a telemetry or voice communications system. Repeaters receive a signal on one frequency and retransmit it on a second frequency.

Repeaters may be fixed or mobile (carried in the emergency vehicle). Many systems employ both fixed and mobile repeaters. Repeaters are useful for extending the transmission range in hilly and mountainous areas, as well as for extending the range of portable transmitter/receivers. In both cases, the primary hardware (the patient-side radio) transmits the signal via the repeater in the vehicle; the signal then is retransmitted to the base station.

Remote console. The remote console is a control console connected to the base station by telephone lines. It allows use of the base station from another location such as a hospital emergency department.

The remote console both receives voice and telemetry signals from the field and transmits verbal messages back through the base station equipment. Remote consoles usually contain an amplifier and a speaker for incoming voice reception, a decoder for translating telemetry signals into an oscilloscope trace or readout, and a microphone for voice transmission.

Encoders and decoders. The dispatch center, ambulances, and hospitals in a communications system all share a small number of radio frequencies. Radio receivers on the same channel would be activated by every message if signals were not directed by the transmitting individual to the desired recipient. The encoder and decoder are the means by which incoming messages are directed to the desired recipient.

The encoder resembles a telephone dial. When a number is dialed, the encoder transmits a pulsed tone; the number of pulses equals the number dialed. All receivers operating on that frequency receive the pulsed tone. However, each receiver responds to only one pulsed code, which is its own three- or four-number address code. When this code reaches the receiver, the decoder opens the receiver's audio circuit. The encoder-decoder system does not prevent other users from listening in, but it does keep them from receiving unwanted messages.

Telephone. In addition to radio communications, many systems employ hard-line (telephone) backup to link fixed components of the system, such as hospitals, and fire and police services. Telephones can also be patched into radio transmission through the base, station ox through manual control at the CCC. This can allow communication between paramedics using radios in the field and physicians using their telephones at home. Although some telephone lines are already provided with amplifiers to insure a strong, undistorted signal, line clearing may be required at individual locations.

Radio Communications: Voice and Telemetry

Radio frequencies. Radio frequencies are designated in cycles per second. One cycle per second is defined as a hertz. The following abbreviations commonly are used:

hertz (Hz)	=	1 cycle per second
kilohertz (kHz)	=	1,000 cycles per second
megahertz (MHz)	=	1,000,000 cycles per second
gigahertz (GHz)	=	1,000,000,000 cycles per second

Radio waves are part of the electromagnetic frequency spectrum, which is assigned for different purposes. Different frequency bands have different properties. In general, higher frequency bands have a shorter transmission range but also have less signal distortion (interference and noise).

Emergency medical communications use both the very-high-frequency (VHF) band and the ultrahigh-frequency (UHF) band. The VHF band extends from about 30 to 175 MHz and is divided into a low band (30 to 50 MHz) and a high band (150 to 175 MHz). The low-band frequencies have ranges of up to 2,000 miles. However, these ranges are unpredictable because changes in atmospheric conditions sometimes produce "skip" interference that results in patchy losses in communication. The high-band frequencies are almost free of skip interference but have a shorter range. Specific frequencies in the VHF high band have been allocated by the FCC for emergency medical purposes.

The UHF band extends from 300 to 3,000 MHz. Most medical communications are in the 450- to 470-MHz range, which is free of skip interference and has little noise (signal distortion). The UHF band has better building penetration than VHF. The UHF band, however, has a shorter range than the VHF band, and UHF waves are absorbed more by environmental objects like trees and bushes.

Both VHF and UHF communication use frequency-modulated (FM) equipment rather than amplitude-modulated (AM) equipment. (Citizens band radios, in contrast, are AM.) There is less noise and interference with PM than with AN equipment.

The FCC assigns frequencies and has set aside frequencies on both bands for emergency, radio communications. A special set of 10 channels (paired frequencies) for EMS communication allows substantial channel space and great flexibility of use for voice and telemetry.

Biotelemetry. The term "biotelemetry" refers to a technique for measuring vital signs and transmitting them to a distant terminal. When the term "telemetry" is used in emergency medicine, it usually refers to transmission of an electrocardiogram (EKC) signal from the patient to a distant receiving station. In the EMS system, EKG telemetry is multiplexed on a normal voice channel using a subcarrier of 1,400 Hz, which may result in minor degradation of the voice transmission over the same channel. The hospital must be able to communicate with the paramedic while biotelemetry is in progress.

The EKG signal consists of low frequencies (100 Hz and less). Radio modulation techniques (in particular, FM) exhibit decreased responsiveness below 300 Hz. To avoid distortion, the EKG signals, are coded into a higher frequency using a reference audio tone of 1,400 Hz. The 1,400-Hz tone then is, modulated by the EKG signal for radio transmission. When the transmission reaches the distant terminals, it is amplified and demodulated to produce a signal voltage exactly like the original EKG signal.

Distortion of the EKG signal by extra spikes and waves is called "noise." This interference can result from the following conditions:

- Loose EKG electrodes
- Muscle tremors of the patient
- Sources of 60-cycle alternating current such as transformers, power lines, and electrical equipment

- Weakening of transmitter power due either to weak batteries or to transmission beyond base station range

Use of frequencies in a system. Assigned frequencies are used in different systems. In a simplex system, portable units can transmit in only one mode: (voice or telemetry) or receive only voice at any one time; such systems require only a single radio frequency. When a network uses two frequencies simultaneously, it is referred to as duplex. Another alternative is to combine, or multiplex, two or more signals so that they can be transmitted on one frequency at the same time.

Unit 2. Communications Regulations and Procedures

Federal Communications Commission

The FCC is a national regulatory and controlling agency. It assigns frequencies and licenses individuals and communications systems. In addition, the FCC establishes and enforces communications regulations.

To enforce its regulations, the FCC monitors frequencies and performs road checks. It also spot checks base stations and their records.

The FCC has offices throughout the country. All communication plans must be coordinated with these field offices. The EMT-P's should be familiar with FCC regulations.

Protocols and Communication Procedures

Standard operating, procedures (SOP's) are necessary to insure appropriate and efficient use of the medical communications system. Standard procedures eliminate unnecessary communication that could overload communication channels. By providing a structure, for essential communications, SOP's make it possible for the physician to quickly receive information about a patient's condition and rapidly transmit orders for the patient's care.

The possibility of misunderstood messages is reduced with SOP's. When these procedures involve coded messages, all persons using the communication system must understand the code and use it properly. These individuals include paramedics, dispatchers, physicians, emergency department staff, and others directly involved in radio communications.

Dispatch Procedures

The dispatcher gathers, information about the emergency, directs the appropriate vehicle to the scene, and advises the caller how to manage the emergency until help arrives. In addition, the dispatcher monitors and coordinates field communications. While performing these duties, the dispatcher must con form to FCC guidelines.

Information gathering. The dispatcher usually collects information by asking a short series of questions. When a call for an ambulance is received, the dispatcher records the necessary information as rapidly as possible. If tape recording equipment is available, a tape should be made of each call to serve as a backup record.

The dispatcher should obtain the following information:

- Phone number of the caller. This allows the dispatcher to contact the caller for more information (e.g., if the rescue team is unable to find the address and needs better directions). Asking for the caller's phone number also reduces nuisance calls because prank callers usually are reluctant to give their phone numbers. In addition, the phone number can help the dispatcher determine the caller's location if the caller (e.g., a traveler calling from the highway) is unfamiliar with the area.

- Name of the patient (if known). This information will help the rescue team to identify the patient.

- Exact location of the patient, including street name and number. The dispatcher must obtain the proper geographic designation (e.g., whether the street is East Maple or West Maple) and the community name, since nearby towns may have streets with the same names. If the call comes from a rural area, the dispatcher should establish landmarks, such as the nearest crossroad or business, or a water tower, antenna, or other easily identifiable landmark that will help the rescue team to orient itself.

- Nature of the patient's problem.

- Specific information about the patient's condition. (Is the patient conscious, breathing, bleeding badly, or in severe pain?)

- Whether the emergency is a highway accident. If it is the dispatcher should obtain the following additional information:

  -- Kinds of vehicles involved (cars, trucks, motorcycles, buses). If trucks are involved, the dispatcher should ask what they are carrying to determine the possibility of noxious fumes.

  -- Number of persons involved and extent of injuries. Even if the caller can only guess at this information, it can give the dispatcher an idea of the size of problem

  -- Known hazards, including traffic dangers, downed electrical wires, fire, submerged vehicles, and so forth. Information about these hazards allows the dispatcher to contact other agencies that will need to become involved, such as the utility department to deal with downed wires.

A special, preprinted form can help the dispatcher obtain all the necessary information and can provide a record of the call. Figure 14.2 provides a sample of such a form.

Dispatch. After the dispatchers receive the necessary information, they should ask callers to wait on the line. Dispatchers then must make several decisions.

- What is the nature of the problem? Is it life threatening?
- Are paramedics needed?
- Are support services needed (police, fire, heavy rescue)?
- Which crew(s) and vehicle(s) should respond? This decision will depend on the nature and
- location of the call and on which units are available. Thus, the dispatcher must know, the status of every area vehicle and crew in order to decide which to dispatch.

In order to make these decisions about medical emergencies, the dispatcher needs training in emergency medical care. The Division of Emergency Medical Services of the U.S. Department of Health, Education, and Welfare recommends that EMS dispatchers receive the same EMT training as the medical crews that they dispatch. The Department of Transportation has developed a special curriculum for dispatchers.

Records. Either the EMT-P or dispatcher or both should record key times for each call. This information should include the times that the call was received, the vehicle began the run, the crew arrived at the emergency scene, the crew left the scene, the patient reached the hospital, and the vehicle and crew were back in service.

10

Date _____ Log No. _____

TIMES

Call received _____ am./p.m.
Car out_____

Arrived at scene_____
Left scene _____
Arrived at hospital _____
Back in service _____
Patient's name _____
Address _____
City/town _____

PATIENT STATUS

Conscious _____
Breathing_____
Bleeding _____
Other _____

If vehicular accident:

Number and kinds of vehicles involved:

_____ Cars _____ Trucks _____ Buses _____Other

Number of persons injured _____

Extent of injuries _____

Are persons trapped? _____

Hazards:
_____Traffic _____Wires down _____ Fire _____ Hazardous car
_____Unstable vehicle _____ Debris _____ Submerged vehicle

Caller: Name _____Phone No _____

Vehicle dispatched_____

Crew _____ Other units called _____

Figure 14 .2. Sample dispatch record form.

Relaying Information to the Physician

Radio communications between the EMT-P's and their physician directors should be brief and accurate. To insure that information is transmitted in a consistent manner and that nothing significant is omitted, the paramedic should follow a standard procedure for relaying patient information. Such information should include:

- Patient's age and sex
- Vital signs
- Chief complaint
- Brief history of present illness
- Physical findings

    - State of consciousness
    - General appearance
    - Other pertinent observations

The following is an example of a concise, informative transmission for a patient in congestive heart failure:

> We have a 53-year-old man with a pulse of 130 and regular, blood pressure 190/120, and respirations per minute. He is complaining of severe shortness of breath that wakened him from sleep and is worse when he is lying down. He has a history of high blood pressure and takes Diuril at home. He is alert but in considerable distress. He has rales and wheezes in both lung fields. We are sending you an EKG.

The above transmission takes less than 30 seconds but efficiently provides the physician with the information needed to rapidly dignose the problem and order appropriate treatment.

In contrast, the following dialogue can be considered:

EMT-P:	We have a patient with a pulse of 130, blood pressure of 190/120, and respirations of 30. We are sending you a strip.
Doctor:	Fine, but what's his problem?
EMT-P:	He's short of breath.
Doctor:	How long has this been going on?
EMT-P:	Just a minute. (Pause) He says it woke him up from sleep about an hour ago.
Doctor:	Does he have any underlying medical problems?
EMT-P:	He takes medicine for hypertension.
Doctor:	Is he in any distress?
EMT-P:	Yes, he's having a hard time breathing.
Doctor:	What do his lungs sound like?
EMT-P:	Just a minute. (Pause) He has rales and wheezes all over.

This type of communication obviously is less efficient. It wastes time and annoys and frustrates everyone. Information should be gathered at the scene and organized clearly in the EMT-P's mind before the physician is contacted. The reporting procedure can be written on a card posted in the vehicle or on the transmitter, so the paramedic can refer to it when reporting in.

<u>Techniques</u>

Radio communications equipment varies from manufacturer to manufacturer. Therefore, the directions in this section are general, rather than specific. These directions must be supplemented with more specific instructions for the equipment in use.

<u>Use of a mobile transmitter/receiver.</u> The EMT-P should:
- Turn unit on
- Adjust squelch
- Listen to be sure airways are free of other communications
- Hold microphone far enough from the mouth to avoid exhaled air noise
- Push the push-to-talk button, and pause before speaking
- When calling another unit, use its call letters first, and the sender's second
- Follow these guidelines when using the radio

    -- Use an understandable rate of speech
    -- Do not talk too loudly -- Do not hesitate
    -- Articulate clearly
    -- Speak with good voice quality
    -- Avoid dialect or slang
    -- Do not show emotion
    -- Avoid vocalized pauses (such as "urn," "uh," "hmm") -- Use proper English
    -- Avoid excessive transmission

- Use the call sign to let others know the transmission is completed

<u>Use of a portable transmitter/receiver.</u> Use of a portable transmitter/receiver is similar to use of a mobile transmitter/receiver. Since the antenna on the portable unit is not fixed in place, however, it must be kept vertical while in use so that the signal can be properly transmitted to the vehicle. From the vehicle, the signal can be transmitted to the base station.

<u>Use of a digital encoder.</u> The EMT-P should:

- Turn unit on
- Adjust squelch
- Listen to be sure airways are free of other communication
- Select address code to be dialed
- Dial selected numbers
- Hold microphone far enough from the mouth to avoid exhaled air noise
- Push the push-to-talk button, and pause before speaking
- Call dialed unit
- Use the call sign to let others know the transmission is completed

<u>Transmission of patient assessment information and telemetry.</u> The EMT-P should:

- Turn unit on
- Adjust squelch
- Listen to be sure airways are free of other communication
- Hold microphone far enough from the mouth to avoid exhaled air noise
- Push the push-to-talk button and pause before speaking

- Call physician either directly or through a relay system
- Connect or attach electrodes to telemetry transmitter
- Follow local procedure for relaying patient assessment information
- Activate telemetry transmitter for the minimum amount of time required by the receiving physician (approximately 15 seconds)
- Verify physician's reception and quality of transmission

GLOSSARY

dispatch: To transmit calls to emergency medical, services and to direct emergency vehicles, equipment, and personnel to the scene of a medical emergency.

duplex: A radio communications system employing more than one frequency.

Federal Communications Commission (FCC): The Federal regulatory agency that assigns radio frequencies and licenses individuals and communications systems.

frequency: The number of periodic waves per unit of time; radio waves are expressed in cycles per second.

frequency modulation: A method of converting an analog signal, such as an electrocardiogram, into a tone of varying pitch that can be transmitted over the radio.

gigahertz (GHz): A unit of frequency measurement equaling 1 billion Hz; indicates frequencies of 1 billion cycles per second.

hertz (Hz): A unit of frequency measurement; 1 Hz equals 1 cycle per second.

kilohertz (kHz): A unit equaling 1,000 Hz; it indicates frequencies of 1,000 cycles per second.

megahertz (MHz): A unit equaling 1 million Hz; indicates frequencies of 1 million cycles per second.

multiplex: In a radio communications system, a method by which simultaneous transmission and reception of voice and electrocardiogram signals can be achieved over a single frequency.

noise: Extra spikes, waves, and complexes in the EKG signal caused by various conditions such as muscle tremor, 60-cycle alternating-current interference, improperly attached electrodes, and out-of-range transmission.

patch: Connection of telephone line and radio communication systems making it possible for police, fire department, and medical personnel to communicate directly with each other by dialing into a special phone.

repeater: A miniature transmitter that picks up a radio signal and rebroadcasts it, thus extending the range of a radio communications system.

response time: The length of time required for the emergency medical services team to arrive at the scene of an emergency after receiving a call for help.

simplex: A communications system that can transmit only in one mode at a time, or receive voice transmissions only.

telemetry: The use of telecommunications for automatically indicating a recorded measurement at a location different from the measuring instrument, such as an electrocardiogram sent from an ambulance and received at a hospital.

UHF band: The ultrahigh-frequency band; refers to the portion of the radio frequency spectrum between 300 and 3,000 MHz.

VHF band: The very-high-frequency band; refers to the portion of the radio frequency spectrum between 30 and 150 MHz.

Made in the USA
Middletown, DE
15 January 2022